Before I Knew Me, You Gave Me a Mirror

Insights and Inspirations

By Jerry Gaines

Edited by Sue Mihalick Rowdon

Cover photo credit Rob Fleenor, Virginia Beach, VA

Published by Jerry Gaines
First Edition

Table Of Contents

Dedication

As a lifelong educator and coach, I also played many other roles --- counselor, minister --- surrogate parent. The most poignant, however, was that of "student." This book is dedicated to the thousands of charges --- my former students and athletes --- who (likely unknowingly) taught me so much about what it means to be a human being.

~ Dr. Jerry Gaines, Jr.

Foreword

It can be said that wisdom is most likely to be found at the complex intersection of intelligence, experience, and insight. As a psychology professor, college administrator, and mental health professional with numerous academic degrees, more than three decades of experience in the "real world," and a strong sense of self, I am thrilled to introduce readers to a book that is chockfull of wisdom from a person who epitomizes intelligence, experience, and insight... Dr. Jerry Gaines.

I first met Dr. Gaines when I was a junior in high school. I was a student in his Spanish III course. I had to wait until Spanish III to meet him because he was so popular among the students that I was not able to get into his overfilled sections of Spanish I and Spanish II when I tried to register. I wanted to take his class because I had heard many positive things about him... but as I was to eventually discover, the most truthful thing I heard, was that he "taught students more than Spanish... he taught students about life."

Once I got into his class, it did not take long for me to realize why he was so popular. From day one, he made me feel important and capable. Even as a relatively passive student at the time, he made me feel seen and heard. It was readily apparent that he did the same for many other students. As an adult, I reconnected with Dr. Gaines via social media, and as a result, I have discovered that he has connected deeply and personally with thousands of others during his career as an educator, coach, and mentor. He appears to have mastered the ability to nurture relationships which are genuine and mutually beneficial.

This collection of his insights and experiences is a personal exploration of the intricate threads that make up the human existence. It boldly and honestly delves into the topics of love, aging, racism, teaching, coaching, mentoring, relationships, and encouragement. This book takes the reader on a genuine and heartfelt journey that highlights our shared humanity... all through the eyes of a person who possesses keen insights, and personal and interpersonal awareness.

Love and relationships serve as the foundational themes of this book. With a healthy dash of self-deprecating humor, the author navigates the challenges of aging. His book encourages us to appreciate the beauty inherent in every stage of life. Through the material, we gain a greater appreciation for resilience in the face of hardship. We are encouraged to seek a life of relevance and meaning throughout.

~ Dr. Darrin Campen, December 2023

Epigraph

Scientists say it takes about twenty-five years for the average human brain to fully develop." We come into the world not knowing very much. We can't walk or talk. We can't even recognize danger. Birth is a ticket to a train ride --- a "knowledge train" that takes us on a fantastic voyage called life. It's important to pay close attention.

We spend the early years soaking up the sights and sounds of life. During the trip, it is critical that we learn to differentiate the "good" from the "bad." Indeed, after about twenty-five years, we should have enough information stored away in our now fully developed brains to knowingly share what we've learned with others.

It is interesting to note that learning never really stops. The older we get, the more experience we have; the more experience we have, the wiser we grow; the wiser we grow, the more we have to share. When life is done properly, human beings should morph from sponges to sprinklers."

~ Dr. Jerry Gaines, August 2023

Editor's Notes

After years of reading Jerry Gaines' posts about relationships, life, racism, current events, and any/everything else, I realized the importance of organizing his "musings" and making them available to a wider audience and generations to come.

Our friendship of more than 50 years enabled me to select from his thousands of musings the ones that are "Pure Jerry" not only reflecting his thoughts but also inspiring the reader.

~Sue Mihalick Rowdon, December 2023

RELATIONSHIPS

Life's Safety Nets

Hugs are absolutely wonderful therapy. Today, find somebody who's hurting (it won't be hard) and hug him/her. It will benefit you too.

· · · · ·

Isn't it amazing how the best relationships don't really require a lot of words?

· · · · ·

Hearts that are deeply wounded are often the very ones that are willing and capable of helping soothe and heal others.

· · · · ·

Inflation, gas prices, the economy, politics, corruption, mass shootings (violence) --- there's always a huge bag of migraine headaches trying to take root inside your weary head. If and when they do, you mope, gripe --- complain. Others always seem eager to share theirs too. Everyone has read the pamphlet --- "How To Cultivate The Perfect Headsplitter." Still others specialize in doling out high-grade, migraine fertilizer. It seems complaining is everybody's favorite pastime. There is only one best answer, and it is found only in the hearts of friends and loved ones. So grab a bunch of them for yourself. They are so needed nowadays. In fact, take two each morning before your day starts (with a tall glass of water). They don't mind.

· · · · ·

Just got one of those "out-of-the-blue" calls from an old friend. His wife and I were teachers; he and my wife were RN's at a local hospital. His kids (2 sons and a daughter) were all fine athletes, and today, contribute positively to this world --- first-responder, educator (Teacher of the Year), and caregiver. We spoke a while about those good ol' days. He lost his beloved wife --- my dear friend --- a few years back (cancer again), but we sure made a bunch of wonderful memories and talked about the endowment they now have in her honor. His name is Bob, and together, I think we made a difference in things.

· · · · ·

As you age, so do your relationships. Time enhances some, and causes others to fade, but time also offers opportunities to create more --- your choice. When the bulk of your marathon has been run, you realize some in the race pass you quickly --- run ahead and leave you, never looking back. Others run alongside you for a while, but after a few miles, they too slowly pull away. Many drop off --- fall away. You can no longer see them, but you dare not search too long, or you could lose your own way. Naturally, you remember most the ones who run with you for a while --- those with whom you shared life rhythms: feet hitting the pavement, breathing --- heartbeats. Today is a good time to stop and think about your running partners. No worries: they'll know who they are.

· · · · ·

The same bricks that build mansions can also build prisons.

· · · · ·

Are you a GOOD FRIEND ---- to ANYONE? The definition of the term may vary somewhat, but the recipe usually remains the same and includes the same precious ingredients: availability, sacrifice, patience, and understanding, but you can easily think of others. Interestingly, playing the role well is as beneficial to the friender as it is to the friendee ---- very often, even more so.

· · · · ·

How many times have you looked back and realized how much TIME and PLACE ---- CIRCUMSTANCE ---- affected the DECISIONS that you (and others) made --- decisions that changed the entire trajectory of your life? (You're probably pondering some of them right now.) Imagine the possible outcomes --- what MIGHT have been. Call it luck, destiny, divine intervention --- what if...?

. . . . .

I confess that I envy the innate, powerful, nurturing instincts of women. That "mama bear" response is very real --- not just to protect, but also to comfort. Little ones crying never fail to garner their attention; it's true sometimes even in animals.

. . . . .

FACEBOOK: It may seem trivial (or maybe even silly), but one of my greatest joys in life these days is to be able to share a great variety of thoughts with a great variety of people on a great variety of topics on a great variety of occasions for a great variety of reasons and to have those thoughts resonate with a great variety of them. I suppose that's why there is such a great (and growing) variety of EMOJIS!

. . . . .

We are all born young. We can only "look" until time and experience produce the wisdom that enables us to "see."

· · · · ·

Above all other goals in life, we must seek to make a positive difference in the lives of others.

· · · · ·

"Close," but not "together;" seeking only "sight" rather than "IN-sight." Apply as/if you see fit.

· · · · ·

Make it a resolution to make lots of people CRY this year --- HAPPY TEARS!

· · · · ·

Statistically, 12% of the population claims to have NO FRIENDS. This might explain the serious uptick in cases of poor or declining health --- physical, mental, and spiritual. So, 88% of us have the opportunity to better the world (and ourselves) by becoming a friend with someone we have not even met yet.

· · · · ·

When it comes to growing up being "cool," most will say they were some of the most UNcool, lame --- nerdy --- kids in school. (You can think of other terms.) But it seems SOME OF THE MOST UNCOOL KIDS DO AN ABSOLUTELY AMAZING JOB OF RAISING THE COOLEST KIDS! You're thinking of a few right now --- probably including yourself. (It's okay to brag a little about that one.) So, when we think of "cooler," IGLOO and YETI should NOT be the first names that come to mind.

· · · · ·

It is perfectly alright to demand --- DEMAND --- a "price" for your friendship if that price is measured by honesty, integrity, respect, and the like.

· · · · ·

I know some (living) people who, were I to reach out and embrace them right now, would actually bring me to tears --- tears of joy just to see and touch them once more.

· · · · ·

By now, the numbers run into the thousands. It's a personal perspective, but over the years, the best thing about Facebook has been seeing the zillions of photos of my kids' kids (young people I taught or coached) growing up and doing great things. Nothing in my world brings me greater joy than watching my former charges learn the ins and outs of life, and they have done an absolutely SPECTACULAR job of raising so many championship kids. It is fascinating to witness the development of their parenting skills (often on the fly, but nobody is perfect). They take on all the inherent challenges, make proper "adjustments," and often surprise themselves when the outcomes turn out better than they ever expected. Through all the doubts and hiccups, they have done incredibly well, and I couldn't be more proud. Now, some of my great kids (who have raised even greater kids) are raising the (my) greatest GRANDKIDS! Change the world? Make it a better place? Heyyyyy!

· · · · ·

Especially during these difficult times, I like to create what I call "backdoor opportunities" for myself. It is no secret that I have a passion for fishing (any kind). Given the chance, I'd drop a line in a ditch, a mud puddle, or your drinking glass if you're not looking! Sometimes, it's good to keep a few to give away to people who love (and may now NEED) them. That's almost as much fun as catching them (but not quite). What to do when the fish aren't biting? Well, I can always bring them a couple of their favorite donuts --- "backdoor opportunities." They're great therapy.

· · · · ·

What's the big deal with just "squeezing" another human being anyway?

· · · · ·

Imagine standing in some huge, open space. In front of you, standing in line, shoulder to shoulder, are ALL of your favorite people in the world --- all awaiting their turn to give you a big hug (for no particular reason). You get to take all the time you need, but no matter how long, imagine how YOU'D feel once you got to the end of your line. You'd probably just go skipping off like some little kid who just received a huge lollipop (those of you who can still skip).

· · · · ·

Are you one of those who take daily nutritional supplements: vitamin (pick a letter) --- A, B, C, D, Q, Y, Z --- or a number --- 1, 2, 3, 12, 36, 547? How about that treasure trove of MINERALS --- magnesium, copper, zinc, chromium, silicon, gold, silver, coal? (Goodness, you could sell your body parts to some mining company!) After years of intense research, an effective, centuries-old remedy has been identified --- the supplement of supplements --- the most complete health-building, life-sustaining product ever found, and best of all, it's free to all subscribers! "What about daily dosage", you ask? Unlimited! Everyone, children to senior citizens, can take as much as they like, whenever they want (no prescription required)! It is all-natural, lab-tested, highly absorbent, pleasant tasting, soothing to the smell, and has incredible brain and cardio-pulmonary benefits. Is it a pill, capsule, tablet, caplet, powder, liquid, cereal, aerosol spray? Nope, none of the above. Every day, simply reach out -call, text, message, write letters, send cards, gifts, visit, hug, kiss --- "TOUCH" one or more individuals you care about (pets count). The results are usually immediate and literally off the charts!

· · · · ·

You can't count the tears you routinely see people shed these days, sometimes your own are mixed in. It takes a high degree of coldness to remain indifferent TO them, no matter the reason FOR them.

· · · · ·

Imagine a boxer with Ali's quickness and Tyson's power. Now imagine climbing into the ring with him. Blows, hard ones, countless ones, land from every direction --- sometimes in combination; some you never even see coming. Many people are feeling like they have done just that these days. These are not times for petty (or any other sort of) squabbles. We have never needed each other more.

· · · · ·

Have you ever noticed how athletes embrace family members, teammates, and sometimes their competitors, after a hard-fought victory? Sometimes there are tears of great joy, and sometimes there are tears of utter disappointment. When human beings embrace each other, for whatever reason --- on whatever occasion --- they should ALWAYS hug like that.

· · · · ·

Even under the most normal circumstances, life makes it essential to surround yourself with as many loving, caring individuals as possible. Naturally, family comes first. Then come friends, some of whom often become like family. Then, countless opportunities to create more present themselves among those we meet along the journey. Viewed honestly, our lives center around THERAPY. Whether we are the providers, or the ones needing it, one thing becomes clear. Whether we choose to admit it, take advantage of it, or not, we desperately need each other. Those who, for whatever reason, do not accept this truth are the ones who create most of life's biggest challenges --- the ones who cause most of the problems.

· · · · ·

After years, fears of disease, COVID, have finally eased. We feel safer about large gatherings: travel, reunions, shopping --- various entertainment venues. We've watched the heartwarming meetings --- those "surprises" --- some not having seen each other for years. The hugs are tighter, longer, and most often accompanied by tears aplenty, even from the "toughest" among us. We ARE better together. Whatever your resolutions this year, that's a good place to start.

. . . . .

No one really comes out and says it, but when offspring are born, we stare at them in awe and disbelief, but we're thinking, "LOOK WHAT WE DID!" Graduations --- when they walk across that stage? EXACT SAME THOUGHTS/EMOTIONS!

. . . . .

When your kids grow up, graduate, and move out, the level of pain you feel is the surest indicator of just how great a job you did raising them. Lots of you know this weird emotion well --- JOY/SADNESS --- it's quite a GOOD thing.

. . . . .

More than most, I post all sorts of things: usually messages of encouragement, inspiration, and reflection. The list of friends who respond to those posts is often wonderfully predictable --- says a lot about my list of friends.

· · · · ·

Many don't think about it. Most are unaware of it, even as it occurs, because they don't realize they can do this with their eyes too, but there are tremendous advantages to becoming a good LISTENER. Along with the many valuable bits of information that can be absorbed from others, you get to know their HEART, while enhancing your own.

· · · · ·

Each of those you call a "loved one" --- family member, friend, casual acquaintance --- is unique, one of a kind. Yet, no matter how many you have, you love each in a different way, for different reasons. More people should subscribe to loving. It is the most wonder-filled and truly fascinating concept.

· · · · ·

If your teenage child's friends loved to hang out at your house, most likely, you were one of the good ones.

· · · · ·

You can collect real estate, money, or antique this or that, but nothing --- absolutely NOthing --- is more precious than your RELATIONSHIPS. THAT'S where your real treasure --- your MEMORIES --- reside.

· · · · ·

Like herding animals or some insects, human beings are SOCIAL creatures. Generally, we do better in groups. Like antelopes, horses, bees, or termites, we can benefit each other in a number of ways, but we are unique in the variety of ways we can appreciate and love each other. It is a special gift that is there for the taking. Life's ultimate goal should be similar to that of a prospector working in a mine, or a rushing stream. The great hope is to one day strike it rich. The challenge, however, lies in having to sift through tons of rock, and "fool's gold", before we can scream "EUREKA!" Most often, gold is found one nugget at a time --- precious because of its rarity --- its beauty. It won't be found by only searching along well-worn paths and railroad tracks. You must dig, pan --- work --- for it, and though the work is hard, the reward is great. Odd thing about gold --- the best way to FIND it is to BE like it.

· · · · ·

Have you ever noticed how easy it is to discern those on social media (in day to day life) who epitomize intelligence, patience, understanding, kindness, wisdom, and a whole host of other wonder-filled traits? I call them "heart people," and like a great white shark, I "feed" on them. They are delightfully delicious and incredibly nourishing.

· · · · ·

Every once in a while, you may be blessed enough to encounter one --- a server, a cashier, or maybe a customer service representative --- "little people" who make their customers/clients feel like BIG people. Being nice to ALL of them is the best way to grow little ones into big ones (that includes you).

· · · · ·

It's definitely not a favorite pastime for many, but I simply love sifting through areas with lots of stones in order to find those unusual (size, shape, color), interesting, truly beautiful ones. You can always find at least a few if you look hard enough. Unlike four-leaf clovers, whose beauty eventually withers away, their beauty lasts forever --- for as long as you want to keep / CHERISH them. To this day, I keep a huge and growing collection of them --- some I could just put on a shelf, pedestal, and stare at for days. It occurs to me that the people I've met in my life are like that. I've read countless posts about all sorts of things – some, more important, some, less important, some challenging, some enlightening – some, truly INSPIRING. I often find myself sifting through them in order to find those unusual, colorful, interesting, truly beautiful ones. You can always find at least a few if you look hard enough. Unlike four-leaf clovers whose beauty eventually withers away, their beauty lasts forever – for as long as you want to keep – CHERISH them. No matter where – no matter the level of difficulty involved – it is ALWAYS worth the effort to find them and squirrel them away somewhere in your heart. In life, they come in mighty handy.

· · · · ·

It's usually desirable to perfect certain skills but learning to cope well with the loss of loved ones is an exception. After all, those most skilled – most experienced – are the very ones who have suffered most. You've been there – just a thought.

· · · · ·

Pizza tastes better when it's shared.

· · · · ·

Just for today --- Father's Day --- I am going to forego the usual quote. Instead, I will copy the words from the card my kids (Jina, Jeri, and Jon) gave me. Naturally, it means a lot, and a shout out to all you other fantabulous dads out there --- younger and older; you know who you are --- that I have come to know during my journey. You have been an inspiration to me in ways you could never even imagine. "THANK YOU, DAD...For teaching great life lessons...like making the best of each new day, sharing what's in your heart, doing the tough work with a smile, and standing up for what's right. Thank you for giving us the skills to last a lifetime...and to make a happy life." Would you understand if I said, "I can die now?"

. . . . .

Those who know best realize life is like those giant roller coasters --- the ones with all those terrifying names. You're probably thinking about some of their names right now. They include tremendous highs and devastating lows. As best you can, it is wise to help others during your high points because you will need that help yourself when it's your turn to descend (screaming and kicking) into your own dips, twists, and valleys. Let's all hold hands.

. . . . .

Fame? It won't matter how many people know that you lived. What will matter most is how many people cared.

. . . . .

In many ways, the earth, with its oceans, lands, and atmosphere --- is like a giant circulatory system.

• • • • •

College students, soldiers, and senior citizens are among the many who are likely familiar with the term --- CARE PACKAGE. These little "love parcels" can contain anything from letters (scented?) to baked goods to toys and other personal items --- little surprises, always cherished. It's heartwarming when someone even thinks fondly of you --- remembers your birthday. It's such a simple gesture. Sending such a package can make a person's day, week, month. Recipients get so excited to RECEIVE them that they don't stop to think about the joy it brings to SEND them. There is something good --- even therapeutic --- about caring about each other. Parents care about their children, children care about their parents, teachers care about their students, coaches care about their athletes, businesses care about their customers, and nurses, about their patients. The list goes on and on. The mutual benefits are as powerful as they are obvious. Perhaps that's why we take the idea of caring so much for granted. Interestingly, we fail to see the (equally ominous attacks on that "one-derful" aspect of the human experience. More and more, people have begun to care less and less about each other --- sometimes even about THEMSELVES. Mass shooters, for example, are quite willing to throw their lives away, opting to spend the rest of their days in prison, or worse yet, to take their own lives. Young people who aren't cared for/about often head off to school where, as a result, they may care little about themselves, no self-esteem. So, failure becomes the expectation; life becomes meaningless. Negative consequences --- poor academic performance or penalties for unacceptable behaviors --- are less and less of a deterrent, educators can identify. It seems that "nobody but me" thinking has become "not even me" thinking. It boils down to a simple matter of whether or not YOU choose to CARE.

· · · · ·

We should value RELATIONSHIP above all else in life. This key life ingredient is at its finest when there is a generous supply of F.A.T. (Faith And Trust) to feed it. Be it between family members, good friends, co-workers --- humans and God --- without generous amounts of faith and trust, the lights never turn on --- people can never see. With all that we know today, it is sad that our nation remains as polarized as it is. The truth, about each other, has been revealed; myth, for the most part, has been exposed. Shouldn't we be much better with each other by now? Relationships are too skinny --- woefully deficient in F.A.T. Everybody is being taught to mistrust everybody, even those in whom we should have the most faith and trust --- parents, doctors, pilots, law enforcement, attorneys, leaders, politicians --- and people -families, communities, nations-are starving to death because of it. KWASHIORKOR, MARASMUS anyone?

· · · · ·

Try to remember the most famous people of your lifetime. It won't matter how old you are --- the most popular kids in your high school or college, entertainers of some sort, sports superstars, or even politicians. Subconsciously, their fame often leads us to believe they'll "live forever." Perhaps, that's why we are so shocked when they pass away, as they all inevitably do. Even the fondest memories, in time, WILL fade away. Everything about our earthly lives is temporary, but while you're here, it's a good idea to make great memories anyway.

· · · · ·

Watching the docuseries, "Life Below Zero," I never knew people "canned" things like fish (halibut, salmon), and meats (caribou, bear) to sustain themselves during those inevitable hard times. It must be nice to simply reach up on a shelf and grab a nourishing, life-sustaining jar during the winter when it's dangerous to even step outside. We should look at our RELATIONSHIPS like that.

· · · · ·

Just had breakfast with a former student --- Marine and college educator. He's in town --- drove hundreds of miles just to comfort a friend who recently lost a family member. He cares a lot --- always has --- but it costs to care. That was one of the first things I told him, and the last thing I said to him as we said our goodbyes. He was here to comfort a friend, although, for the past few years, life has really been beating him up badly. He hadn't been home for a while, just wanted to sit and small talk a bit --- updates on families, memories of old friends, some now deceased. He reminded me of how comforting home smelled. He remembered, and since he was close, he realized he could use a band-aid. I have lots of them and was happy to share. When he drove off, his smile was sincere --- not like the forced one I saw earlier. He's gonna be okay. He cares.

· · · · ·

When you show up, words are rarely necessary.

· · · · ·

Most would agree that RELATIONSHIP is foundational to life and happiness --- the stuff that actually makes life worth living. All of nature is proof of this. Yet, that one key factor is being systematically removed from the equation of life --- family, education, business (banking, industry, sales), politics, and virtually every aspect of day-to-day living. We are gradually, unconsciously --- literally --- being "weaned off" of each other, direct human interaction. Isn't that why people find phone trees so exasperating? "LOOK, I WANT TO TALK TO A PERSON!" Didn't COVID teach us anything? How can this possibly end well?

. . . . .

Call it weird, but maybe it's not such a good thing that society seems to be systematically removing the simple act of 'human touch" from the equation of life. From the moment we take our first breath, 'til the moment we take our last, we need --- indeed crave --- this simplest, most human gesture of kindness, tenderness, kinship, and yes, of love. Sadly, like so many other simpler treasures of this life, we have taken it --- bent and twisted it --- until, sadly, it has been oh-so-quietly reduced to nothing more than attempted acts of debauchery. That is truly sad.

. . . . .

JUST A FEEL-GOOD STORY: A few days ago, I was inside not doing much of anything when I heard this loud noise outside. I live on a main street, so I thought there may have been an accident. I rushed to the front door to find my mailbox some distance down the sidewalk from its original location. This was the 3rd time. A young man in camo fatigues was approaching me from my neighbor's driveway where he had stopped. He looked to be about 20 or so, and as it turns out, was one of our local sailors. He shook my hand and was very apologetic about having taken out my mailbox --- an extremely nice kid. His name was Kyle. He offered to buy another --- even to help me install it. I said, "no, it's not the first time. I'll take care of it, and you can pay the replacement cost. I'll keep the receipts and call you when I'm done." We exchanged numbers. Now, four days later, Kyle shows up at my house. He brought along his wife, pregnant and due any day, and his mother-in-law, here for a month all the way from Bremerton, Washington, for the birth of their first baby (it's a girl). We had a most delightful visit --- absolutely WONDERFUL people! We sat in my living room and chatted for more than an hour like we were old friends. They live just around the corner, and you couldn't know a finer family. By the way, Kyle is actually 28 years old --- definitely OFFICER material. He's based here but is from Ohio --- has a Buckeye tattoo on his calf, wearing shorts on his return visit.

· · · · ·

Many people you encounter each day live lives that scream (in no uncertain terms), "IT'S ALL ABOUT ME!" In a different sort of way, this post is just that:

In all the many roles that I have been "summoned" to play in this life, I have always tried to be "good." For as far back as I can remember, even to age 4 or 5, I tried hard to please. I tried to be a good son; I tried to be a good student; I tried to be a good athlete; I tried to be a good friend; I tried to be a good soldier; I tried to be a good educator; I tried to be a good coach; I tried to be a good husband; and I tried to be a good father. Because I am only a human being, I realized early on that I would not, COULD not, play even one of these roles perfectly. I was (still am) hopelessly flawed --- quite needy --- in each. How does one deal with so many obvious shortcomings?

· · · · ·

This holiday season is a good time for me to share with you just how THANKFUL I am that the desire to do good --- to BE good --- was there in me, and I'm not exactly sure where that desire came from. Was it from my parents? I'm sure they played a huge role in it. Was it from the many mentors who did their best to lead me down the "paths of decency?" I'm sure they played a huge role too. Was it all in God's divine plan? Yep, of that I am most certain. At any rate, it was a most important revelation when I realized how each and every one of YOU played such a key role in the making of "me." I couldn't possibly write down all the names! You made countless critical contributions to my growth, my development, my belief system --- everything! And each of you came along at just the right time --- just when I needed your particular, precious, contribution most. Of ALL things, I need to be most grateful for that. I AM deeply grateful for that. I realize the process is ONGOING. There will be others --- valuable new faces, who, like you, will come into my life soon --- today, or tomorrow perhaps --- and I can't wait. Anyway, may you have the happiest ever Thanksgiving and entire holiday season.

· · · · ·

If you think for a moment about the personal memories you and I have created/shared in this life, then you may have some idea about the wonder-filled role you played in making me. Thank you.

· · · · ·

Don't believe in miracles? If you've met me, you've seen one. I believe in miracles mainly because of each and every one of YOU that I've met. How could I not?

· · · · ·

I see you. I am here. Powerful words.

· · · · ·

Many will agree that adolescence is a fascinating stage in life. Of course, some can think of more "colorful" modifiers. Lots of changes, physical AND mental, can occur during those few years. Teenagers come in an endless variety of flavors, but if observed closely enough, "boring" will never be one of them. And while much can be said about their "peculiarities," there is one thing that teenagers do particularly well, no matter the grades on their report cards. Adolescents are the world's greatest decipherers of insincerity, phoniness --- crap. It is a huge no-no to not be "real" with them. They have an uncanny ability to perceive whether or not a person really CARES. Convince them that you do, takes longer for some than others, and you can win them for life.

· · · · ·

Know what? I think MEMORIES are terribly underrated.

· · · · ·

Spoke with an old friend today. Just speaking with him generates emotions similar to those I get when I reach for my favorite fishing rod.

· · · · ·

Just saw a term on a tv commercial that bears repeating --- certainly worth sharing: DADICATION.

· · · · ·

Lost another former student today --- cancer, again. Just had an amazing chat (messaging) with his twin sister. This guy was one of the most unusual kids I ever met --- truly one-of-a-kind, truly brilliant. Most of his teachers didn't care for him very much because he could read every one of them, including me, like a book and had the moxie to tell them what he thought. His story was a long, twisted, yet fascinating one. We talked often. He'd be riding his bike to some job, see me cutting the grass, and stop to chat. We must've saved the world a thousand times right there in my driveway. Along with his entire family, I will miss him a lot. Right now, his sister and I just needed to swap bandages.

· · · · ·

If you truly love someone with all your heart, soul, and mind, you have gifted that person with the best of who you are --- ever could be. You cannot do better than that, but if you are blessed enough to find one who is willing to return such a love...(it's not even necessary to finish the statement).

· · · · ·

Why always "US vs. THEM?" Why not "us AND them?" Why not simply "US?"

· · · · ·

Many wonder why we should go to such lengths to maintain relationships with as many friends and acquaintances as we can, but that's where the treasure is; that's where LIFE is. There is no higher priority. Any other pursuit --- ANY --- is merely existence.

· · · · ·

I've got opinions and viewpoints about everything, and I'm not too shy to share them. I stress relationships because, from them, we get those precious memories. For that reason, I was moved to stress one more thing. To the best of your ability, ALWAYS try to keep FAMILY first and foremost in all you do. The rest will take care of itself. That's all.

· · · · ·

TRUE friendships are the perfect insulation against FALSE ones.

· · · · ·

During the last months of his life, I drove my brother to Richmond for his cancer treatments. I became familiar with every curve --- every tree --- along that hundred-mile stretch of I-64. Particularly poignant were the makeshift memorials --- those little white crosses, sometimes with flowers, that marked the sites where someone's loved ones lost their lives in previous accidents. Sitting and waiting for his treatments to be completed, 4 to 7 hours usually, things often got quite lonely, but this was my brother. Privilege --- honor, sacrifice --- humbling --- come to mind. During those 90-minute trips, we saved the world dozens of times, never once discussing the fact that he and I had already accepted the inevitability of things --- thoughts of miracles having long since faded. My brother is doing fine now, but what I remember most is how so many dear friends came over to sit and share in the loneliness of the most grueling sessions. While my mind struggled with "those thoughts," THEY were there --- the best therapy. I cannot forget their patience, kindness, and generosity. I'm sure that, were it possible, many more would have done likewise, you know who you are. Sometimes, "thank you" doesn't seem quite enough.

· · · · ·

Can you remember a time when you simply had to walk away from so many people?

· · · · ·

Happiness is to getting what contentment is to giving.

· · · · ·

If someone cuts you, the deeper the wound, the longer it takes to heal. Stitches and antibiotics are sometimes essential, but if for whatever reason treatment is denied, it can lead to infection, gangrene, and amputation. For YOUR sake, forgive.

. . . . .

So tiny and vulnerable, what is it that makes hummingbirds so bold? They routinely fly within inches of total strangers, look them in the eye --- perch on a finger at a first meeting. The tiniest creatures can sometimes teach us the biggest lessons --- if only we would listen.

. . . . .

One of life's most profound truths: "If you truly care, it's going to cost you, and those who do are forever willing to pay the price."

. . . . .

Meeting someone for the first time should always be viewed as an investment.

. . . . .

Do you remember going on family vacations as a kid? Oh, it didn't really have to be the "sophisticated" kind where you packed camping / beach --- whatever --- gear, and preparations sometimes took days. It may have been a much-looked-forward-to weekend, or just a day spent in your family's "special place." Those were fun times, for sure, but what is it about THIS time of year that makes it so special --- so unforgettable? THANKSGIVING, after all, marks the beginning of that extended, end-of-year celebration that just naturally includes CHRISTMAS. Of all your memories, what is it about these two that never fails to stamp indelibly in your brain all those wonder-filled times and events that ever bring you back, no matter your age, to childhood days back in... back when...? For some of us, snow was a magical bonus, but it was hardly necessary.

• • • • •

More than any others, these two celebrations conjure up descriptors like "heartwarming" and say "togetherness" like no other. Indeed, families come together to share turkey and pie, of every description, but more than anything, to share EACH OTHER. Can't you just see Aunt Mary, or Grandpa Joe walking up the driveway to your front door now? You were watching through the front window, so their arrival was never a surprise. Aunt Mary was carrying that foil-covered, favorite dish, she always said she made it just for you, and Grandpa Joe was so loaded down with brightly wrapped gifts, he could hardly see where he was going. Perhaps there were games to watch --- games to play --- or just the anticipation of catching up on the events of the year --- births, first teeth / steps, graduations --- conversations going on everywhere, and nobody appearing to be really listening. Then, grandma, or some other high ranking, "traditional delegate" would call all the celebrants, young and old, together around the table. And just for a moment, the home became "magical" --- lights dimmed, the air heavy with a thousand aromas, the "quiet" of the moment, spellbinding, and the little ones looking up at all the big faces --- eyes closed, heads bowed. Someone (you already have a name) was usually charged with saying a special blessing --- not just for the food this time, but for everyONE, present (and absent). There was the celebratory carving and the slicing and the handing of all those deliciously fragrant things around the table. You always ate too much, then piled "just a taste" of two or three desserts on top of it all --- gloriously stuffed for hours afterward. You clearly remember Uncle Josh always had to loosen his belt a notch. You will (can) never forget.

• • • • •

It is about the RELATIONSHIPS --- family, and friends from everywhere: college, office, down the street, or maybe even an occasional, total stranger, but it's always about the PEOPLE --- some of whom, if we're honest, we occasionally may have taken for granted. During these two holidays, we concern ourselves more than ever with the "US-ness" of this life. THAT, is the MAIN reason you do not forget! Don't fail to "gather yourselves together" this holiday season, and do remember those who may not be so blessed. Celebrate the LIFE that each of you brings "to the table" (all year long) so that, over time, as those "special chairs," one by one, "go vacant," you will know a deeper meaning behind yet another of the "why's" of life. Love them all now! BLESSINGS, and ENJOY!

· · · · ·

I'll bet you know people who, when you give them some small "happy-nothing-in-particular" gift, feel they simply MUST reciprocate (when that's not really the idea at all).

· · · · ·

Memories are reminders of the inevitability of change. Remember your home, your street, your neighborhood, your city, state --- the nation --- when you were little? Huge difference, huh? Nothing is the same; nothing stays as it was. To the extent that we can, it is our responsibility to make sure the changes we make are treasured. The best way is through the way we affect change in other people (starting, of course, AT HOME).

· · · · ·

Another "date" with a former student yesterday --- not over a meal in some nice restaurant. This one took place at the end of her brand-new pier --- a lovely place on a local river. Knowing my love of fishing, she invited me over to "try it out." The scenery was breathtaking --- wide river with miles of forested shoreline on the far side. The day was hot, but she had a boathouse (with Adirondack chairs) out on the end --- beautiful. At long last, she had returned home. She married a wonderful guy, she, an oncology nurse, and he, a successful engineer. They have two fine sons --- both college grads, at least 6'5", and former athletes. She was anxious to tell me how happy she was to finally be back home. After years in Colorado, she wanted to be close to her elderly mother, and there was no more threat of forest fires. I, justifiably, repeatedly, praised her for her "mommy skills" --- hers, a near-perfect blend of toughness and tenderness (so rare these days). They had raised those two sons . . . very well. In fact, she introduced me to one of them --- a fine young man, no surprise. He was home for a short while before moving back to Colorado to accept a position in computer technology there. She, too, is one of my great kids who raised GREATER kids. Like so many, she was one of those who just flew through high school without making any waves. Great moms often use possessive pronouns when they speak their kids' names --- "MY_____" , a dead giveaway. It makes sense that good moms often make great nurses. And yes, we caught three different species of fish, including a couple of stingrays. She was surprised that "croakers" are appropriately named --- like frogs, they DO croak. Of course, we released them. Yesterday wasn't about "catching." Then again, maybe it was. Those goodbyes are always long, but God willing, I'll be back when the "predator fish" move up that shoreline in the fall. Of course, she gave me an open invite.

．．．．．

I don't know all the thoughts that run through the minds of those in nursing homes, or those languishing in hospital beds. The minds of a good number of them might remain sharp, but day in and day out, many can only lie there, looking out of windows or counting ceiling tiles. That's why they cherish personal visits so, from anyone. Understandably, they have an enhanced appreciation of TIME. Even a visit from a nurse or custodian is welcomed. But a visit from one whom they have loved in life, and especially from one who has loved THEM, is priceless. There is a powerful lesson to be learned here. Every year, I am blessed to receive a bunch of heartfelt birthday wishes from many whom I sincerely love, and from others who have (for whatever reason) loved me. They are tonic --- the stuff that keeps me upright and willing to continue that "fight for right." If you are a late starter, you may want to begin gathering, hoarding, as many of these people as you can. Keep them close. It won't matter whether they live there in your home or halfway around the world. You will be lifted to a new level of humility and gratitude.

. . . . .

Thought of my fishin' buddy today --- wished he could be here to see some of these magnificent sunsets. Silly thought.

. . . . .

At one point or another in your life, you have probably won some award, or managed some achievement that meant a lot to you. It may have been something as mundane as passing a test, or something as fantabulous as winning a Super Bowl ring. At the moment, you may have even shed tears of joy. But when all the tears dried, as they do, when all the cheering subsided, as it does, when everyone went home, and you were left to look back in the rear view mirror at that special moment, your "victory," however cherished at the time, PALES by comparison to those indelible moments in life that you shared with SOMEONE TRULY SPECIAL to you --- a spouse, a child, a teammate, a roommate, a fellow soldier, a colleague, a neighbor --- perhaps that "special friend" whose life path just "happened" to cross your own. It is only when, if, you come to this realization that intelligence morphs into WISDOM --- when you realize people --- RELATIONSHIPS --- matter more than anything. It is that moment when you should ask

35

yourself, "Why WOULDN'T I want to MULTIPLY these feelings --- this JOY?" By comparison, all those trophies you hang on your walls, or place so neatly on those shelves in all your special places --- all the glittery trinkets and souvenirs of past accomplishments --- mean little to nothing.

· · · · ·

Hugs are absolutely wonderful therapy. Today, find somebody who's hurting, it won't be hard, and hug him/her. It will benefit you too.

· · · · ·

There's a very real war being waged. While most are convinced that loving, caring, and sharing are great tools for building relationships, others are equally convinced that the best way to treat others is in the worst way.

· · · · ·

A good friend: sometimes, you have the most wonderful phone conversations. At others, you might enjoy an impromptu lunch after having unexpectedly found a little free time in the middle of your day. Eye contact is infrequent --- unnecessary really. Each of you knows the other is listening intently --- always. However, it's those very intentional times when you're sitting comfortably together, most often staring out at nature --- water, mountains, trees, saying absolutely nothing, that is the most powerful therapy of all --- the perfect backdrop as you quietly view all the old videos --- those precious memories that brought you so close in the first place. May you have/be such a friend. You don't/won't get many; you don't/won't really need many. Each one is the biggest lottery win ever.

. . . . .

Wild horses can be beautiful. At first approach, though, you just might get a vicious kick. Feral dogs can be beautiful. At first approach, though, you just might get a vicious bite. Stray cats can be beautiful. At first approach, though, you just might get a vicious scratch. Treated patiently, kindly --- lovingly --- each can eventually become a model of loyalty and devotion --- a TRUE FRIEND for life. We seem to have forgotten; this works particularly well with PEOPLE too.

. . . . .

How many people do you know right now who, had YOU not been there at the exact moment that you were, their lives might very well have run completely off the rails, or ended altogether?

. . . . .

Sometimes when the world has grabbed you by the scruff of the neck and is shaking you all around, thoughts of a close friend can loosen its grip like nothing else.

. . . . .

"Thee-minded" or "me-minded" --- far too many lean toward the latter."

. . . . .

As any veteran spouse will tell you, no matter how long you know the person you marry, they will always have a few "surprises" for you AFTER the wedding --- things about them that you never knew, things about which you had no idea at all. With some exceptions, this is a GOOD thing --- as it should be --- but one point should be emphasized here. Forty years of marriage is plenty enough time to discover both a spouse's strengths and "shortcomings." Not to sound conceited, but I am capable, albeit RARELY, of some acts of PURE GENIUS, if I do say so myself. More often, though, I am at least TWICE as capable of acts of incredible STUPIDITY, especially now that I am a bona fide senior citizen. Some of you will immediately understand; others, just wait! Anyway, years ago, when I did dumb stuff, sometimes for fun, other times because I honestly couldn't help myself, I asked my wife to ask herself to consider --- prioritize --- my MOTIVE(S) above my METHOD(S). I call it the "M & M Principle." She was quickly able to deduce that I hardly EVER did anything with any malicious intent. This made my frequent forays into total mindlessness more FORGIVABLE. If she had problems with that, it wasn't MY issue. The problem was mine only if I meant to do harm. But why would I do that? After all, to harm HER is to harm ME, and that would be the STUPIDEST of things. That one realization did wonders for our relationship as we continued to grow together, and most importantly, provided valuable lessons that we, to this day, share with our kids. Oh yeah, she's STILL learning stuff about me, and I'm still discovering more than a few new things about HER too! When I look at it honestly, it's all quite fascinating.

· · · · ·

How many "negative" statements have you heard about this past year --- 2020? It certainly brought more than its share of challenges, didn't it? But if RELATIONSHIP is the most important aspect of the human experience, then 2020 has been an unexpected, eye-opening blessing --- yes, blessing --- for most likely, it also birthed in us a deeper, clearer, more powerful appreciation of and for EACH OTHER. Amid all the complaining, back-biting, stabbing, conflict, disagreement --- negative stuff --- there has also been a heightened level of empathy, generosity, kindness, and understanding --- positive stuff. I call them "back door blessings" --- GOD stuff actually --- those life episodes that seem tragic at first, then somehow, turn out to be true awakenings. It's Christmas time, and this year especially, you feel it --- appreciate it --- even more than the smell of live Christmas trees. Because it taught us so much, this year became a time of LESSONS, and lessons, though sometimes painful, are always good. Whether you wanted to or not, you were reminded to slow down, to think, and to appreciate the simpler things --- food, family, friends, a warm fire. Yes, 2020 brought with it a year's (decade's?) worth of lessons, and despite all its ills, social media taught us that we are still learning --- perhaps better and faster than we realize. Once all the dust settles, and don't be deceived by the background noise, more of us will be committed to making this a better world. We have learned more about this life --- about how to best appreciate each other --- and that's the best lesson of all. BLESSED HOLIDAY WISHES TO EACH AND EVERY ONE OF YOU!

· · · · ·

Not a single day goes by where I am not reminded of the many, wonder-filled individuals I have been blessed to meet in this life. Many of those chance encounters, combined with all the very "intentional" ones, have become treasured lifelong relationships. They have made me among the richest human beings. You already have quite a few yourself.

Knowing there are people like that in this world, we need not focus on the minority of sad ones. Instead, we should remain eager to carefully seek out even more of those great ones. There are always more of them than it appears. It's also the best thing we can ever do for ourselves.

· · · · ·

Think about the people you've met in your life --- all of them. Some, you may have met only a few times (maybe just once), but there are some out there who have this "power." They can be any age --- any demographic --- and without really trying, they can touch your heart in amazing ways. Almost immediately, you just feel close --- drawn --- to them. They have this aura (some of them truly glow) that may be there in their eyes, their smile, or in the sound of their voice. Without a word, they can convince you that life is, indeed, worth living. (Hopefully, you married one!) When you're having one of "those" days, they are better than any therapy, or your finest meds. In your life, I sincerely hope you have found a few. There are never enough of them; they are certainly worth finding, and keeping. Life is a lot like working in your own diamond mine.

· · · · ·

As surely as there are interactions between human beings, disagreement and conflict will be inevitable.

Relationships can be wonderful, but for any number of reasons, they sometimes sour, and before one or the other decides to reconcile, almost always an option, one might unexpectedly pass away, leaving the other feeling a terrible sense of guilt. Sadly, too many know that feeling too well. Reconciliation, forgiveness, is powerful, and for good reason, it comes highly recommended.

· · · · ·

Hateful people know neither peace nor happiness. They eliminate the need to even mention hope.

· · · · ·

Social media can be a great way to get, or stay, in touch with family and friends or to create precious new relationships, worldwide. With photos of offspring, travels --- even pets --- you can brighten the days of as many as you wish --- known and unknown. You don't really have to search very long to find something that will make you smile either, but oh-so-quietly, a few out there who poison those placid waters by seeming to get joy out of creating chaos --- wreaking havoc by contaminating others with their bitterness. "Trolls" is a good term for them. No doubt, you are familiar with their tactics. They hide under their bridges, jump out and throw their rocks and rotten vegetables at passersby --- those just happily trying to get across. Imagine that. Trolls can be found in check-out lines at stores, you might have encounters with them in parking lots and a host of other venues, but it seems they invade social media in force. There seems to be so many more of them these days too. It's exhausting to have to deal with them. I think that's why pets have gained such unprecedented popularity in recent years. They never throw rocks and rotten vegetables, and they are quick to forgive. Spreading kindness is therapeutic, and a whole lot more fun too. Do it for yourself then. Learn a lesson from your pet or a family member or a friend or some new relationship out there.

• • • • •

Not long ago, I was invited to speak to the inmates at a huge regional prison --- maybe 60 men and approximately 30 women. It was one of the most amazing experiences of my life. Not surprisingly, there was no shortage of tattoos on faces, necks, and arms. I admit I hurried a bit to finish my spiel. I wanted to get to the Q & A so I could discover more about "who" they were. The stories were humbling, and heartbreaking --- not exactly what I had expected. They were remarkably gentle, caring, loving, brilliant --- HUMAN. I have never left a presentation feeling so desperately sad, but I suppose that was something I needed to experience. I could see their faces --- hear their voices ---

the entire ninety-minute drive home. I was back in my old element --- my classroom, and the practice field.

· · · · ·

Do yourself a favor. THINK about that person in your life who was a great TEAMMATE, and it need not involve sports at all.

· · · · ·

As surely as we take our first breath, we will one day take our last. We all know this. Along life's journey, we get to witness any number of arrivals and departures (scheduled and unscheduled). Each should be a lesson to us --- one that far too few ever learn, and far too many totally disregard. By learning to LOVE (the lesson of lessons), we generate all those great RELATIONSHIPS that produce all those great MEMORIES that are foundational --- the very makings --- of all those great LIVES.

· · · · ·

Have you ever been the source of JOYFUL tears? Great feeling, isn't it? Those memories are easily remembered and always deeply cherished.

· · · · ·

RELATIONSHIPS are the stuff of life. It's interesting how genuine fear (terror) is being generated in all the places where large groups gather: schools, kindergarten through college, places of worship, all faiths, shopping, convenience stores to malls, sporting events, amateur to pro, theaters, live and movie, concerts, parades --- workplaces. Was Darth Vader onto something?

. . . . .

There's a bunch of people in your life --- not necessarily in your immediate circle --- who (were they there with you right now) would hug you so tightly and for so long that you'd have to catch your breath afterward. Think about them. Can't you smell their neck? I just did, and I'm just catching my breath.

. . . . .

People sometimes refer to "a brother from another mother," or "a sister from another mister." You may have met as early as elementary, or other school, or at work. Such individuals teach the true meaning of FRIENDSHIP. Sometimes, sadly, life moves them to faraway places, but the memories --- those memories --- remain as fresh as they were the day they were made. Great relationships are therapeutic; they mean something and should be cherished. After all, "reunion" means "coming together again as one."

Most likely, you're thinking of someone right now. Today might be a perfect day for a reconnect.

. . . . .

Every culture throughout history has discovered its share of remedies for all sorts of ills. Today, television is forever promoting some new drug, the side effects, often worse than the disease. But when all is said and done, there is no better cure for what ails ya than A TRUE FRIEND.

. . . . .

Oooo, ahhhhh, oh wow! How often has one of those eye-popping, jaw-dropping, scenes in life left you gawking --- speechless? You probably have favorites: mountains, forests, clouds, beaches, seascapes, sunsets. Fairytale scenes can actually pop up anywhere --- in your backyard or in a quick glance from an aircraft window. There can be wonder in both natural, and man-made scenes --- mesmerizing things to behold --- cathedrals, castles, palaces, monuments --- ancient, hauntingly beautiful places that can fill you with awe and wonder. But you don't really need to travel the world to be blown away by amazing things. The most amazing things in life aren't things. Stopping to smell the roses means realizing that PEOPLE are the roses! So many of them are every bit as worthy of your awe and amazement as any mountain (or fountain) --- very genuine miracles.

You just have to be careful sometimes when you reach in among the thorns to pick one. They come in all shapes, sizes, and colors. And with a little cultivation, they'll grow just about anywhere.

· · · · ·

Those who have no appreciation for life (in all its many forms) have to be the loneliest people in the world. Conversely...

· · · · ·

ULTIMATE GOAL: To make as many as you can care that you lived.

· · · · ·

Stationed abroad, incarcerated, or otherwise assigned, confined, or maligned in uncomfortable environs, it is wonderfully comforting to receive notes and letters from friends and loved ones. It's like they send along pieces of themselves too --- always deeply moving. When you receive those little life savers/preservers, they are immediately precious, cherished, and often squirreled away to reread later. Instinctively, you press them to your face, and sometimes you SMELL them, allowing your mind to take you to their origins --- where they were penned --- "home." Interestingly (and still unbeknownst to many), the absolute best therapy --- the finest cure, for whatever ails us, --- is US.

· · · · ·

From the time I was a little boy, like everybody, I made everything about ME --- what I felt, and what I wanted. Slowly, almost imperceptibly, I realized what I really wanted (needed) in this life was to be happy --- surrounded by as many happy people as possible. It made sense to make it a primary goal (for my own sake) to make others happy. After all, I had control (albeit limited) over that. Through the years, I was given more hats to wear --- roles to play, but in every venue, the same thing held true. In my educational pursuits, career aspirations, entertainment --- whatever I did --- I was better (felt better) if my focus remained on helping others. Of course, fatherhood provided a fresh, wonder-filled world of opportunities for that, so I dove headlong into that role as well. (In the process, it enhanced my "husband hood" skills too.) With one child or six, the same thing held true. Each was a unique opportunity to create (create) new ways --- to offer a little more light --- to a sometimes-dark world. Success here was particularly invigorating, exciting --- inspiring --- and I could apply those same principles to EVERYBODY! I discovered that's where "success" morphs into "significance." Far from perfect, I will always have something worthwhile to strive for, but I've had some incredible role models (older AND younger). I still take a lot of notes, in fact. Happy Father's Day to all you fabulous dads out there (and to all you fine role models!) Humbling...

．．．．．

Some endure a lot of hatred and pain in this life, and end up hating and hurting others, and yet, some take that same cruelty and hurt and find ways to become some of the kindest and most loving people on earth.

．．．．．

Ever given any thought to the critical role that "harmony" plays in the human experience? Everything has a "harmony element": atoms, the human body, parenting, family, music, positions on an athletic team, corporations, organizations, education, clubs, neighborhoods, societies, cultures, religions, politics (yes), nature, weather, the earth, inner space, and outer space as well. It seems obvious that if we (no matter the reason) decide to interfere with, disrupt, or disregard this harmony factor, especially when it comes to establishing healthy, HARMONIOUS relationships with each other and this universe that we all call home, we ultimately condemn ourselves. Harmony simply must be the "good stuff" we all seek/crave in life. It's a goal we should all pursue in all that we do. It may sound unrealistic --- fantasy, "pie in the sky" --- but isn't this what we really seek not only during holiday seasons but all year long?

. . . . .

When you were very young --- when you took your very first "baby steps" --- you likely had an impressive supporting cast all around you. Your parents, grandparents, siblings, neighbors, and friends surrounded and encouraged you: "C'mon, Sweetie! You can do it! Walk to (pick a name)!" You stumbled and tumbled (usually on your bottom), but somebody was right there to help you back up and urge you on. WHEN you made it to someone's anxiously waving arms, they cheered gleefully, swept you up, hugged you, and spun you all around. Many of the problems children (and adults) face today can be traced back to times when they lost their cheerleaders.

. . . . .

Diamonds come in an impressive array of colors. Their color is due to certain exposures --- heat, certain chemicals, or gases. The 3 critical factors necessary to form diamonds are heat, pressure, and time. No element in nature is harder, yet they are made from one of nature's most common elements --- carbon (crystallized). They are the hardest substance on earth. In fact, only another diamond is hard enough to cut one. And no matter what your jeweler tells you, no two are identical. They are precious but are not really "rare." You already know where I'm going with this.

. . . . .

Sometimes, especially when I'm alone, my thoughts turn to "me" --- how I relate to all the stuff going on around me --- the perfect definition of "musings" I guess.

. . . . .

The phrase "being used" has gotten a bad rap because "to use" is so often confused with "to abuse." In fact, to downplay the importance of being used is to overlook one of the main purposes of our very existence. It's no news; we are all unique --- gifted in some way --- but what is the purpose of all that unique giftedness, and why is there such an amazing, incredible array of human skills and talents in the first place? While most usually derive some measure of joy from their gifts, is its main purpose to please only its owners? Should we not employ those gifts to please others as well? Why is there so much joy in that anyway? You already know those feelings. You even regret not taking advantage of some of the opportunities you've had to share your gift(s) with others. Sadly, such thinking goes contrary to the world's way of thinking. Truth is, it really IS "all about you," but only if your greatest joys in life are based on sharing and gifting yourself to others.

• • • • •

David Lokie was one of the finest human beings I ever met. He also raised two fine kids --- a great dad. Like too many I've known, he was stricken with that scourge we call cancer. It played one of its familiar, cruel games --- made everyone think it was gone, then it returned with a vengeance. During my last visit, I remember him lying there on the couch in his home, Carolina blue basketball shoes there at his side. I invited him to a retirement party that my family and my students were throwing for me. His last words to me were, "I'll try to make it." That was Dave. I'm sure he tried his best, but he missed the party by two weeks. He made me stronger. This life, huh?

• • • • •

It takes COURAGE to care deeply, genuinely, about people --- family, friends, casual acquaintances, total strangers. Those who dare realize that, while suffering and pain are guaranteed, the potential REWARDS make it the most significant of risks. Failure to pick up that one precious gauntlet is nothing short of selfish cowardice.

• • • • •

Sometimes when I write sad things, I can feel all these hearts --- my therapy.

· · · · ·

There have been more than a few happy birthday wishes this year. Nearly all of you already know how that makes me feel. I WILL share a few thoughts about my GRATITUDE (which, for such occasions, will probably not be unlike your own). After all, don't such well wishes say, "We value you --- you're really WORTH something to me?" What better compliment can there be? Family members, friends, and acquaintances from all segments of my life have taken the time to touch base just to let me know they cherish our relationship. For me, probably no surprise again, that is literally "diamonds and gold." For me, it is the amazing ARRAY of people that makes the whole thing so "mind-blowingly overwhelming" --- from those I've known all my life, to relative "newcomers" to my own special version of "Ringling Brothers." At any rate, I am humbled. So thank you. If you took the time, then that says pretty marvelous things about YOU too. I'm sure you are all quite busy "doing life," yet you stop for a moment to offer a little applause for one with whom you may have shared a memory or three. I don't think it can get any better than that. Still, I guess it doesn't hurt to say it again. I thank GOD for each and every one of you, and especially for the very unique and special MEMORIES with which each of you has blessed my life. In retrospect, each truly has been a wonder-filled gift. God willing, maybe I'll get the chance to thank you again about this same time NEXT year! There are sure to be many NEW memories and even MORE FABULOUS events included by then!

· · · · ·

Got another event scheduled --- breakfast with a former student. She and her twin brother were two of my finest. They, their two siblings, and their parents, were some of the most beautiful people I've ever known. Each of the four kids was also uniquely brilliant. Not long ago, the brother passed away (cancer again), and this will be his twin sister's first birthday without him. In celebration, we'll meet at his favorite restaurant. There will be tears this time.

· · · · ·

Finally got to have breakfast with his twin sister. It has been seven months since he left us. For the first time in her life, she celebrated a birthday without him. The hug needed no words. She whispered in my ear, "I promised myself I wouldn't cry," but the tears fell freely on the shoulder of my jacket. She wiped them away. We sat and I listened as she shared, as only she could, the story of his last days --- memories that came alive in this old mind, memories that only she could have known. And I learned, yet again, the relentless nature of cancer and how it can ravage even the strongest, healthiest among us. She showed me the photo of the reflection in the glass of her front door --- his face on the outside, peering reassuringly through at her. Her son saw it too. Then to confirm, as only he could, there was the dream --- the large, legal-sized envelope lying on the floor. The only legible part of the address --- OKLAHOMA. Strange, he had never been to Oklahoma --- never knew anyone there --- until it dawned on her --- a message, typical of him: "OK, HOME." We promised to sit and share more later.

· · · · ·

Isn't it fascinating how certain AROMAS can conjure up unforgettable MEMORIES? You're thinking of a few right now.

· · · · ·

Had lunch with a former athlete of mine today. She recently --- suddenly and unexpectedly --- lost her husband and wanted to talk. I remembered her as a shy teenager --- unusually unsure of herself. Sometimes, even during practice, there would be tears. Nearly all teens struggle mightily at times as they seek some sense of identity, and stumble often in their pursuit of it. This one athlete became a different person as a member of our All-State mile relay team. Oh, the fears were still there, but the presence of her TEAMMATES gave her courage like nothing else, and she ran "angry"--- for them, not wanting to let them down. She keeps in touch with them to this day. Sports helped her to cope with her very real fears back then; they played a huge role in helping her overcome this devastating loss now. After a long hug, there were tears again and smiles anew as we said goodbye and promised to stay in touch.

· · · · ·

It has been said that, though we are IN the world, we should not be OF it. And yet, amid its myriad wonders, and our own insatiable drive to survive/thrive, those wonders often represent a huge distraction. It is easy to lose one's sense of self with the world offering such a ready, generous feast for the senses. We are naturally social creatures, but precious therapy can be found during those times when human beings can get away and be alone. It is during those times that the world and all its glittery trinkets can be forgotten for a while. It is in solitude that human beings most often discover their true identity as well as that of the Creator of it/us all.

· · · · ·

Called an old friend the other day and was disappointed to get only his voicemail. To my surprise, he called the next day, apologizing and explaining how they have phone issues out in the country where he lives. We taught on the same faculty for decades --- hunted and fished together too. We had not seen each other or talked in a long while. Through the years, we had watched each other become parents, then grandparents. We created and shared many special memories, but I remember most a day when we were fishing in a stump-filled cove on a favorite lake. Atop a stump, he spotted a nest filled with wild duck eggs, he said they were mallards. I was a little surprised when he paddled over and, one by one gently removed each egg, and placed it inside his shirt. He could see that predators, snapping turtles, had already destroyed some of the eggs, so (science teacher that he was), he took the rest home and placed them in his incubator. He knew the ducklings would stand a better chance that way. Patiently, he waited; all of them hatched. He fed and raised those little ducklings 'til he felt they stood a fighting chance in the wild. Then, he let them go. I'll never forget the time we spent in the woods, with my Dad, or the many fish we caught, but that "duck memory" remains with me most. Joe is a great friend, but he is a wonderful human being. He lives less than an hour away. I'm planning a surprise visit soon. We have some catching up to do.

· · · · ·

I have noticed something. When I post messages about hugs, loving, caring, and sharing, there are far more "likes and amens", and that's sad. It's as if people are somehow "starved" of these common life commodities. It's as if they can never get enough of them. Each day, we are beaten up, and then down, by the hatred we see demonstrated toward one another. We TALK of peace on earth, but apparently, too few get the message. Certainly, too few LIVE it. Christmas, Hanukkah, Kwanza --- whatever you call it --- those hugs, the loving, the caring, and the sharing shouldn't need a special date to be practiced effectively, should they? There is more than enough bad stuff already. What can you do? Make this holiday truly special by making a gift of YOURSELF. Be creative with it. You already know how. Then, do your best to stay the course year-round. Your world will brighten, and you will be blessed.

· · · · ·

I live on a very busy street. It's not unusual for me to hear horns blowing or voices yelling out of car windows when I'm in the front yard. Yesterday, the shouts came from a pickup truck. It slowed and turned into my driveway. Yep, former student, and now principal of a local intermediate school, taught his wife too. Bear hug --- so glad to see each other. He told me their student/faculty basketball game was being held that evening. The gray has started to appear in his beard. I offered him my Absorbine --- told him how PROUD I am of him (still). We laughed, another bear hug, and he was off to his game. I smiled all the way to the house. Life's simple pleasures are the best.

• • • • •

Try it once or try it a dozen times. Do almost everything right, and the results might be problematic OR wonderful. Do everything wrong, and the results might be problematic OR wonderful. Try your best, be as dedicated as you wish, or don't try at all, be as apathetic as you wish, and the results might be problematic AND wonderful! The challenges can be intense and may appear endless. PARENTING has got to be the most imperfect of sciences AND the toughest job you'll ever love.

• • • • •

Over the years, I have invited some of my former charges --- athletes and students --- to go fishing. It is thrilling to watch their faces (even the veterans) when they reel in a fish, even a tiny one. No matter the age, they grunt and squeal like little kids again. They are "busy," and don't even notice my smiles. It touches my soul to hear them talk about what they've learned in life. They are the salt of the earth. Intelligence plus time does equal WISDOM.

• • • • •

Humans often hate what they don't know. Because ignorance can fuel fear, fear can fuel hatred. Policies that promote polarization and separatism can promote ignorance which (history proves) often ushers in hatred and violence --- a vicious circle. Fear, in the wrong hands, can be a powerful tool/weapon --- a clear by-product of misunderstanding. From the moment you take your first steps, life is a challenge. Everywhere you look, there's always "one more thing." They either weigh you down or build you up. In the face of each, you have a choice. This is why you search so diligently for things in life to CHERISH. You are ever on the hunt for those little things in life that "fuel" you, keep you in the hunt, and help you to endure: a baby sleeping, a porch swing, a warm fire, spring flowers, a brilliant dawn --- a good friend. These are far more powerful --- far more beneficial --- for EVERYONE to get to know one another.

· · · · ·

During my career, I taught and coached thousands of young people. Sometimes, when they post all those photos of the accomplishments of their children, and grandchildren, I ask them, "Did you ever think...?" You can imagine the responses. Recently, I thought about the number of my former charges who have lost a child or grandchild. There were more than I realized. I loved, love, my kids. Some are 60+ now. That was a particularly poignant, heartrending thought.

· · · · ·

A former student dropped by today --- hadn't seen him in thirty-six years. He's been living in California, Oakland area, but happened to be visiting family and, seeing that I had forgotten to close my garage door, something told him to check and see if I still lived here. Always a smart guy, he was very successful, even in that tough, west coast environment. He shared how he had lost the older of his two daughters, complications from a TICK BITE, of all things --- Lyme disease. Not surprisingly, he teared up sharing those last precious moments with his "little girl." She was 31 and loved him like...well...you know. He and his family are planning to move to Capetown, South Africa (of all places). I smiled and shook my head as he drove away --- waving wildly.

LOVE

One + One = ONE

When people live in such a way that they MAKE you love them, they never really die. There is peace in that thought.

. . . . .

Have you ever REALLY loved someone? Have you ever really BEEN loved by someone? Most likely, you have. Love is truly powerful stuff --- arguably the most potent force in the universe. It can generate strength in weakness, emotions where there were none, and like nothing else, inspire a vast array of absolutely incredible feats. After having examined this critical aspect of the human experience for lo these many years, I have concluded that this simply HAS to be the very ESSENCE of the God that so many claim to "so devoutly" seek in this world --- "appropriate," accessible to everyone, everywhere, all the time, and leaving no place or need for any perceived petty differences.

. . . . .

Medical research has determined that as much as NINETY PERCENT of illness and disease is stress related.

These are trying times, to say the least. It's easy to fall victim to stress (in any one of its many forms), but it can be costly to allow oneself to be swallowed up by the negativity that is forever, everywhere, rearing its ugly head. It may sound trite, but LOVING is great therapy. It's free, always worth the effort, and its amazing, stress-relieving, healing properties are world-renowned. *I do not suggest this is always "EASY."

. . . . .

LOVE is a blessed curse. While it adds meaning to life like nothing else, the CARING that it births can cause incredible PAIN in a world that often seems so full of HATE.

. . . . .

The more you withdraw and dispense from your bank account, the lower the balance. Your love account works just the opposite.

. . . . .

As it has with so much else, our culture has perverted the concept of love. As a very famous poet once said, "...let me count the ways." Perhaps he can, but I can't. We love things (and not people). We often confuse love with "lust". Some say they "love" their children when they simply spoil them. And that's just 3.

· · · · ·

When a loved one leaves this world, the most painful part is not so much the "cause" of their departure --- tragic accident, catastrophic disease, etc. That part "ends." It's more the (lasting) fact that you will not see them again in this life. Since they were loved, the sense of loss is more painful. The deeper the love, the deeper (and more lasting) the pain. Since death is inevitable, it should make more sense to NOT love so deeply because that only intensifies --- extends --- the suffering. Yet, above all else, humanity desperately seeks to love (and to be loved) more than anything, making it the most sought-after treasure in life (albeit elusive at times). It is always worth whatever price it takes to experience. If living is loving, then death, as we know it, must be hating. Hatred hastens death. At best, it confuses loving, and at worst, totally destroys it. We can always choose, but it is an amazing, humbling thing to be gifted with someone (anyone) to love. To disregard --- discard --- such a glorious blessing is to waste life --- an absolute travesty.

· · · · ·

In all likelihood, it's not your motivation, but what if you are somehow rewarded for your generosity, somewhere down the line, in some ways you never even recognize? Gifts are nice, but the best of all will forever be LOVE.

• • • • •

True love is really just a perpetual competition where one says to another, "I bet I can OUTGIVE you, and I won't even bother to keep score. That's why/how it never gets old.

• • • • •

When you think about the many challenges we all face in life, simply put, and it sounds so cliche, LOVE does trump them all. The Beatles were right.

• • • • •

There are negative aspects to social media, but there is a good side too. Sometimes, you can fall in love with people you've never even met face-to-face, and probably never will, but that "extra love" can be wonderfully uplifting and give you hope that you might otherwise never know. You know who you are.

• • • • •

Simply put, human beings are at their most wonderful when they love each other.

• • • • •

#1: Remember your impatience as you couldn't wait 'til you turned 21? #2: Remember cleaning out, garage sales, charitable donations, etc. attic, garage, shed, that storage facility and realizing what a packrat you had become? #3: Remember, just for fun, thinking about Christmas, and maybe even snow, on that hot day in July? Then, before you knew it, it was Valentine's Day and there was still a Christmas decoration that you had not taken down. #4: Remember making that last payment --- credit card, vehicle, house? What do they all have in common? TIME! Each of us gets only a limited amount; don't wish yours away: don't waste a single day (rhyme). You already realize, of all life's treasures, time is the most precious. #5 Remember, if you choose to LOVE deeply --- sincerely --- it can be the ultimate journey, for only love has the power to take away the fears that sometimes come with the inevitable passage of time. It's the holiday season, my friends --- just a reminder.

· · · · ·

Have you ever watched the expressions on the face of a new mother as she looked into the eyes of her very first child for the very first time?

· · · · ·

By far, the greatest gift you can ever bestow upon others is to love them.

· · · · ·

The words in this year's birthday card: "DAD, YOU'VE MADE A DIFFERENCE IN MY LIFE. Whether you were by my side, teaching me something new, or just watching TV with me, I always felt important when I was with you. Even when I got older and busy with other things, you still made time for me and found ways to let me know how much I mattered to you. You still know how to make me feel that way, Dad...Because today I know more than ever what a really good man you are, what a great father you've always been, and how lucky I am to call you Dad. HAPPY BIRTHDAY with Love. This has probably happened to you: My two daughters, in two different stores, and in two different cities, chose the exact same card. One of them found it right away; the other poured over every card in the display before choosing this one.

· · · · ·

If you have ever experienced the blessing of being TRULY LOVED in this world, you will not be able to resist the obsession to share.

· · · · ·

Just as LOVE enhances life and makes it richer, HATRED takes it all away.

. . . . .

The lyrics from a very old tune include this wise advice: "Take time to know her; it's not an overnight thing. Take time to know her. Please don't rush into this thing." Of course, you can substitute "him/them" in there. Do you believe in love at first sight? Most often, that one is more myth than reality because it's based more on fickle emotion than tried and true wisdom. We shouldn't be surprised by the predictable outcomes --- failures that usually far outnumber those happy, fairytale endings. Odds are, you have befriended, or even fallen in love with, someone you definitely shouldn't have. Ironically, the solution to this age-old issue is simple --- obvious. Outside appearances are one thing but matters of the heart, what lies INSIDE, quite another. When it comes to quality human relationships, CHARACTER matters --- greatly, always. A GOOD HEART is priceless --- indispensable. Everything else is just window dressing. People are willing to invest vast amounts of time and energy to become great performers on the world's stage, but too many fail to carefully inspect the most critical happiness ingredient --- hearts. Could that be why there are so many unqualified, even corrupt, elected officials, both here and abroad, these days? "Take time to know them; it's not an overnight thing. Take time to know them; please don't rush into this thing." As sure as sunrise, life WILL bring its share of pain and suffering to the table. It makes no sense to raise the odds of their appearance in your life.

· · · · ·

In life, those who never discover LOVE are sure to discover PAIN. As far as suffering and struggle go, life offers, guarantees, a full array. Love is the most effective, only, salve for life's darts and daggers. It puts life's weapons in perspective, cools negative emotions, teaches people to embrace inevitable hardship, and actually increases WISDOM.

· · · · ·

Some years ago, my brothers and I operated a business called K-9 Express. In short, we did exactly what the online pet store, "Chewy," does now --- free, truck, delivery of some of the finest canine (and feline) nutritional products, supplies, and toys. Not surprisingly, we had the best clientele you could imagine! If you've noticed, dog lovers are truly a unique group of people, and quite different from "cat people". When it came to "pet care," nearly all of them did four basic things: 1. If known, they celebrated their pet's birthday --- cake, doggie ice cream (yes), the whole nine yards. 2. They talked to their pets as if they were people, played special music for them, built "special (in-house) accommodations for them too. Many dogs ACTED more like people than most people, and some of the outfits, especially for the toy breeds,...well...Gucci would be proud! 3. At Christmas time, they hung a stocking for the dog too. After all, 'tis the season. 4. And when the time came to take the family photo, right there front and center... It's interesting to note that our clients quite often took better care of their pets than they did themselves. And in a few, hotly, contested divorce settlements, there were some incredible legal disputes over who got the dog. (Some of you are nodding right now.) Those were interesting, fun times for us, and despite the hard work, we enjoyed it immensely.

• • • • •

Once upon a time, dogs had to earn their keep. They usually played dual roles --- pet and guardian, pet and hunter, pet and herder, etc. Now, we lavish love on them like never before, and all they have to do is "be there" (which they are almost always more than happy to do). I can't help wondering if people are turning to their PETS for the love they're NOT getting from other people. You can scold your dog for any misbehavior one minute, and a few minutes later, talk about "forgive and forget" --- and no grudges (usually)! Say what you will, your pets love like all of us should (and too many of us never learn to). So, spoil them rotten; they're worth it. Then, later on, you don't have to send them off to college either.

· · · · ·

PEACE is a near and dear sibling --- not a distant, unfamiliar cousin --- of LOVE.

· · · · ·

How can there be growth without challenge --- victory without struggle? There is often a hidden blessing in the test.

· · · · ·

If you learn to LOVE well, it is ironic that you will also learn to FIGHT well.

· · · · ·

I am not the richest of men, then perhaps I am. In my life, having gotten a little long in the tooth, as folks used to say, I have seen some things --- some that can be described as truly horrific; many that filled me with humbling wonder; and still others that let me know with assurance that, no matter the number of years, life CAN be "worth living." The real value of all those experiences lay in the fact that I have been blessed enough to not simply "look at" this world, but also to "see" it --- to discern those things that matter most. I don't know why I was so blessed --- can't think of anything I may have done to deserve such a priceless gift. I have crossed paths with some people that I can honestly describe as not very nice. You've probably met a few, but I can just as honestly say I hate no one. No matter your life experiences, it is wise to choose LOVE. Of the many things that human beings cherish, I have zero doubt that, in the end, it IS the greatest gift of all.

· · · · ·

Indeed, human beings are "fearfully and wonderfully made," but they are also selfish, and greedy. Dishonesty and violence are preferred choices when it comes to problem resolution. It is impossible to do life alone. For YOUR sake, love others.

· · · · ·

One of the best words to pair with "love" is "now."

· · · · ·

There are many words to describe different things, but "FLEETING" is a rather odd example that usually describes only one. This modifier lends a sense of urgency --- a message that sometimes whispers, sometimes screams a mixed message in our ears, "Hurry, but don't rush!" Importantly, when you give this one thing away, it is the perfect demonstration of loving. Life only offers us a "fleeting" opportunity to love. What will you do with your TIME?

. . . . .

Life comes at us in endless stages; things change. Survival requires adjusting, hopefully with the help of others, while holding firmly onto the hand of LOVE, always there for the choosing. It is the best possible companion to have with us along this twisted way.

. . . . .

It's graduation time again. Prom and other senior class stuff --- graduation announcements, cap & gown, "Pomp and Circumstance" are almost done. Parents are scratching their heads, wondering where the time went and how they got here so doggone fast! Future plans --- be they college, employment (or maybe travel) are set. Parents, especially mothers, are reminded of that day when the nurse first placed your tiny future graduate in your arms. You breathed a sigh of relief then; you breathe an even deeper, longer one now. It has been quite an experience, but you won. A shout-out to all you PARENTS; you don't often get the recognition you deserve. You've done well, and we're CRAZY PROUD of you too!

. . . . .

My life has not exactly been easy, but even at its best, life never is. Since the day I was born, a truly incredible amount of change has taken place, but struggle, in all its many forms, has been a constant companion. It has been terribly burdensome at times, but TIME and EXPERIENCE eventually reveal themselves as the main ingredients in the recipe we call WISDOM. They teach that trials, tests, challenges --- the "issues" of life --- are an integral part of growth. Life will do its best to generate bitterness and wreak havoc; wisdom teaches there is only ONE way to withstand the onslaught --- LOVING.

$$\cdot \ \cdot \ \cdot \ \cdot \ \cdot$$

It's easy to know when love is real; it's the only way one plus one equals one.

$$\cdot \ \cdot \ \cdot \ \cdot \ \cdot$$

No one wants or likes to think about it, but each day, the reality that you could lose someone you know --- someone you love --- is always there in the back of your mind. You might get the news in a multitude of ways as you try your best to steel yourself against the inevitable heart hurt --- usually futile. If you lose someone and it hurts you deeply, it SHOULD. The pain is proof that a person's life had MEANING --- SIGNIFICANCE --- (most likely, for far more people than you). Most likely, they LOVED deeply ---

sincerely --- and in so doing, WERE equally loved. That is the best life anyone can live. Their loss won't (and shouldn't) erase the pain but focusing on that one "love aspect" can bring a smile (if only a weak one) through the tears and those initial moments when you can only sit in silent disbelief, staring blankly into space.

· · · · ·

When you see LOVING, as a verb, you can't help wondering why so many spend so much time and effort HATING.

· · · · ·

Nobody loves people more than those who love to cook.

· · · · ·

Hatred should be avoided at all costs. To hate is to cheat oneself of life's greatest joy --- loving truly.

· · · · ·

For a while now, we have examined the variety of ingredients featured in that wonder-filled cookbook we call LIFE. From its main ingredient, LOVE, to that bitter one that never fails to taint and accelerate spoilage, HATE, we have done our best to become gourmet chefs. Of course, a few of us have suggested adding chili powder to our favorite pound cake batter, but by and large, we have created delectable main courses, delicious casseroles, tasty side dishes, and decadent desserts --- recipes, masterpieces, to die for. And we created them TOGETHER!

. . . . .

In this life, it's a good idea to THANK the people who have truly loved you. They are the best medicine of all.

. . . . .

By comparison, our entire planet is a speck of dust. For that matter, what is our entire solar system compared to all that? And what difference can YOU make? In the whole scheme of things, no matter how long you live, you either choose to love or you don't. That simply HAS to be where the significance lies. What else could possibly matter? Besides, it answers all 3 questions.

. . . . .

I am a little more than six feet tall and weigh a little more than two hundred pounds, but lately, I've been feeling rather small. I've been researching how it takes light, traveling at 186,000 miles per second, 100,000 years to cross from one side of our Milky Way galaxy to the other. .

. . . . .

The largest star, among the 500 billion, in our galaxy is hundreds of times bigger than our sun, and there are countless stars in countless other galaxies that are countless times bigger than that. Additionally, the number of galaxies in the known universe is estimated to be about two trillion (yes, with a "T"). Just try to wrap your mini-brain around that, and you might need a planetary-size bottle of Excedrin! So, what is it that could possibly make the human experience of any "notable" significance whatsoever? It's helpful to remember the size of the universe when trying to find meaning in the few seconds you get to spend on this microscopic speck twirling around in this endless expanse, at about 67,000 miles per hour, mind you. Such thoughts keep you humble, and humility provides a perfect segue into why accepting (and sharing) life's most powerful gift --- LOVE --- is so critically important. Choose LOVE, and amazing, life-altering things happen. Your sense of self-worth is heightened. You stop merely "looking at" creation and you begin to SEE it. You don't hurt quite as much when you attend the funerals of dear friends and loved ones. You are inspired to imagine their "spirit selves" everything that made you love them in this life, "out there" zipping around,even faster than the speed of light, exploring all that endlessness before joyously being welcomed into a place beyond all that where time means nothing. Some say there are "gates" there. Some say you can "feel" the colors there. Some say there are no tears there. Most importantly, some say it's the most wonder-filled place all your dearest friends and loved ones could ever want to be. That must be where all the love in the universe is collected and shared, and it can all start right here, right now, with just little ol' you.

. . . . .

Many people choose hate over love, making hating appear easier than --- preferable to --- loving when that doesn't even make sense. It says a lot about some human beings.

. . . . .

To become a parent is a priceless gift. If every child is a miracle, then every parent is a literal MIRACLE-MAKER. Many of my former students, athletes, colleagues, and friends realize this truth.

. . . . .

Have you ever known "that" couple --- two people who loved each other more deeply than Julio and Romiet? Such love is fascinating, and unlike so many, grows deeper with time, but with time comes the realization that one day, one of them will have to say goodbye to the other. However, something magical always happens when that time comes. "There's nothing more we can do," doctors say, and the vigil begins. But from somewhere, faith begins to build. You've seen this. The faintest smile from the stricken one is reason enough to rejoice. And when the end does come, something amazing happens. Amid the heartbreak, love still triumphs --- a glimmer of light in an otherwise crushing darkness.

. . . . .

Love HAS to be the most powerful force in the universe --- the greatest tool in the human toolbox --- oh, that the whole world could have a taste!

. . . . .

Live long enough, and you WILL eventually experience pain and anguish. In this life, deep loss is as certain as sunrise. It is so common that, on any given day, finding hurting, suffering people is easy, though some hide it so well it may be difficult to tell. That's why kindness is such a good OTC prescription (for everybody). It is a key byproduct --- the most effective remedy --- for life's inevitable wounds --- LOVE. And yet...

TEACHER, COACH, MENTOR

FARMING HEARTS

Young people come into this world as just a pile of shapeless bricks --- all sizes, and colors (a few broken). It's the MORTAR (environment --- mentors, etc.) joining those brittle bits of clay together that matters more than anything. It ultimately determines the size, strength (and design) of the buildings.

. . . . .

It is still an honor – deeply humbling – to be called "COACH" even after having retired decades ago. I have lots of friends who know this feeling well.

. . . . .

It is no news that the responsibilities of any society's EDUCATORS are crucial. Their success is dependent upon their ability to make accurate OBSERVATIONS, and ASSESSMENTS of human PERFORMANCES as they grow and develop. Educators "educate" by dealing with all the complex aspects of LEARNING. Character, work ethic, kindness, and trustworthiness --- those traits that societies cherish --- all play their part in the process. Teaching careers often span decades --- proof positive that, in general, educators love what they do. Education is the ultimate "people" business. Teachers, by default, are in the best position to examine and diagnose human behaviors. As such, people really should listen to what they think --- to what they have to say. Collectively, they instruct, officiate, judge --- lead. They play a huge role in the ways people view themselves, and more importantly, the roles they each play in the world.

· · · · ·

Teachers, coaches, parents, et al, are amazed --- inspired --- when they hear a young person say, "I bet I can do that."

· · · · ·

If you've fished for a while, you've learned just how much goes into it (especially if you want to get really good at it). You might figure "water is water," but there are so many "types": freshwater, saltwater, whitewater, inshore, offshore, topwater, bottom, or mid-depth (suspended), water color/clarity/temperature, tides. And that's just the WATER! It REALLY gets complicated when it comes to BAITS. Factors might include size, weight, color, action & presentation (ask a pro), artificial or natural. There are always WEATHER considerations: temperature, sunny or overcast, humidity, wind (speed & direction). And we haven't even mentioned rods and reels: light, medium, heavy, spinners, level-wind, open or closed face, length, graphite, fiberglass, bamboo. This list doesn't even come close to covering all the factors involved in catching the thousands of different species that an angler might wish to target.

· · · · ·

Think of any basic COLOR; there's likely a species of fish with that color in its name. It is truly amazing to see experienced anglers "work their magic." Any angler will tell you, there's a huge difference between "fishing" and "catching."

· · · · ·

In many ways, professional EDUCATORS are "sophisticated anglers." THEIR tackle boxes are just larger and significantly more complex. All the factors that apply to great anglers, though, apply to great educators. With the circumstances these days, it is deeply troubling that our best anglers are being stripped of much of their tackle, while still being asked to catch the same number, or more, of citation and trophy fish, only now, they're being asked to do so in very dangerous weather, with their hands cuffed behind them.

. . . . .

Is discipline really discipline if the disciplined ignore its intent and continue unacceptable behaviors? A child might be confined to his room, but he might decide to exit through a window. They may be called, "teachers," but is their job really "to teach" or to PRESENT THEIR CHARGES WITH THE OPPORTUNITY TO LEARN? Whether or not learning takes place depends on THEM, doesn't it? Is it a matter of MAKING them learn, or making them WANT to learn? Life really IS a lot about choices.

. . . . .

In many ways, teachers are FARMERS. They water their crops regularly, apply proper fertilizers, and apply pesticides as needed in order to cultivate quality produce for export to world markets.

. . . . .

It is gratifying --- thrilling --- to see former charges, there have been many, wade through muddy, snake-infested swamps, and come out on the other side bloodied and scarred perhaps, but much TOUGHER, having endured and WON!

. . . . .

I have witnessed artisans create amazing, masterful works in wood, clay, glass, stone, on canvas, and some, even on paper --- each, a magnificent work that gave me the chance to take a quick peek into THEIR world. Then, I thought about parents, teachers, coaches, counselors, and ministers, and I was REALLY blown away!

. . . . .

I am old enough now that a good number of the young people I once taught and coached are losing their parents, many of whom I never once met, but because of the children they raised, I am so humbled and grateful that I must have loved those parents too.

. . . . .

I received a post recently that included yet another photo of a high school graduate --- a truly handsome young man who is the son of one of my former student-athletes --- himself, just a fine human being (you'll see). Confidentiality, no names, --- you'll understand. MY MESSAGE: "Another graduate? You're playing this as perfectly as can be played, and I couldn't be PROUDER. You doin' okay?" HIS RESPONSE: "Thanks so much, Coach! This means a lot. I am doing well. Had a bit of a setback with my new treatment, causing some neuropathy issues, but I think we've righted the course there. This living scan to scan takes some getting used to, but still able to squeeze the sh&@ out of these lemons handed to me to keep making the lemonade. So proud of our boys. _____ starts his life in Austin later this summer and looking forward to visiting _____ at his university and catching up with some old college teammates at the games this fall. These graduations have particularly touched my heart because, and I haven't told many folks this, back in October 2019, when I was first diagnosed, and the doctors didn't yet know how far this fast, evasive, and deadly form of cancer had spread. I had a recurring dream for the next 3 weeks. Both boys were graduating, they were given their diplomas, and I am watching and cheering. But they don't see me, and they both just look upward and point up to the sky. They were pointing to me. I didn't make it to see them graduate. And I would wake up in tears. I am just particularly grateful to God that that dream/nightmare didn't play out. I'm still here and will continue to fight for every moment life has to offer. Sorry to spew so much. Last night, it all just hit me. I truly hope you and yours are doing well. Watching all these graduations and successes should make you proud. Because you had a hand in every single one of them! You most certainly contributed to how I am playing this!!!

"There's a bunch of poignant messages in this one. I'm sure you didn't miss them. By the way, this was his follow-up response when I asked him if it would be okay to publicize his words: "If you think it will help someone, anyone, absolutely please feel free! Thanks, Coach --- for everything."

· · · · ·

Great coaches convince you that you CAN get that last glob of peanut butter out of the bottom of that deep jar with that short spoon.

· · · · ·

Good teachers believe in their hearts that EVERY student is GIFTED in some way. That's one reason why it's so hard to get good teachers to give up on even the most difficult of their charges. This one trait should qualify teachers as national treasures. What have we done?

· · · · ·

Parenting can be one of the most wonder-filled experiences imaginable. You cannot make yourself more significant in this life than to help raise another great human being. Teachers get to taste this delicacy every day.

· · · · ·

From Columbine 'til now, there are always stories about how teachers sacrificed their lives trying to shield the kids, even in colleges. If you are or ever were an educator, how do you deal with that?

· · · · ·

Every student who sits in a classroom, every athlete who is ever coached, and every young person ever mentored ALL make the same request: "TELL ME WHO I AM." The response, in one way or another, should likewise always be the same, "I see you; I hear you; you matter."

· · · · ·

Ever wished you could navigate the stock market like the pros? You've probably heard some of the jargon: insider trading, hedge fund, bull/bear markets, commodity, index, liquidity, correction, futures, crash, Rising Tide Lifts All Boats. It can get complicated, but I suppose it's deeply gratifying when an INVESTMENT pays DIVIDENDS. So many fail to realize that a nation's EDUCATION SYSTEM is its actual (and most important) Wall Street. In one way or another, each of those terms above applies.

· · · · ·

Every year, teachers encounter students with a truly amazing variety of problems. Unsolicited, they usually go that extra yard, often digging into their own pockets to help youngsters with problems that many will never see. And while a few youngsters might take advantage of their kindness, teachers don't mind so much. In the long run, kids remember that stuff and sometimes remind those teachers decades later. That, in fact, is the teacher's unsolicited payback.

. . . . .

When you see people begging for handouts at a busy intersection, what's your first thought? "They're just scamming," you tell yourself. You avoid eye contact --- a bit uncomfortable 'til the light changes. You remember the dollar you gave to one of them once. Maybe they used it to buy cigarettes, or maybe drugs (or so you convinced yourself). You hate being flimflammed, but what does their scam really cost you? Who ends up better, or worse, off? You don't have to give anything to anybody. The power to choose is always yours. Check your own conscience. It might be better to roll those dice --- take the chance that maybe, just maybe, their need is real. If they are scammers, they have a bigger problem anyway --- certainly bigger than your being minus a dollar or two. Teachers don't think like that. They can't afford the risks. You don't have to be a teacher to know that, right? If you lose money in an honest attempt to help someone, then it's really not wasted. In a way --- either way --- it's an investment.

. . . . .

Especially when I coached cross country --- distance runners --- victory didn't always mean being among the first to cross the finish line. In many cases, it simply meant convincing young athletes that they could go farther --- harder --- than they ever thought they could.

· · · · ·

As a teacher and coach, I didn't have students and athletes. I had SONS and DAUGHTERS.

· · · · ·

Especially recently, EDUCATION has been an even more controversial topic --- understandably and justifiably so. Life is all about RELATIONSHIPS --- the greater the diversity, the better. That's no secret. Teachers get the opportunity to immerse themselves in a world where they can generate as many as they wish --- students, sometimes siblings, parents, colleagues, foreign and domestic, and a whole host of individuals in a grand variety of arenas. Yet, school systems everywhere are short, by tens of thousands, of qualified educators. Those who are the personification of tolerance and endurance are collectively throwing up their hands and walking away from a career that has forever been "a labor of love." It's unnecessary to say, but teachers DON'T do it for the money, and the culture wars are not really a priority. Currently, 55% are considering leaving the profession. Personally, the countless relationships that I have known, and to this day, still enjoy immensely, have given my life purpose and meaning like nothing else. Those RELATIONSHIPS have placed me among the richest of human beings. Climate change, inflation, crime, and all the others are important, but to overlook, or in any way downplay the importance of education/educaTORS, is a huge, regrettable mistake. You don't have to be a college professor; the signs are already there, and I'm afraid this is only the beginning.

· · · · ·

As a father/teacher/coach/mentor, I tried never to tell young people what they SHOULD be. Instead, it was much more effective to tell them what they COULD be (anything), and the CHOICES were always and ultimately theirs.

· · · · ·

Do you have a favorite sport --- a favorite athlete? Have you thought about what it takes to get that GOOD? Each of us, everyone, is at least as gifted at SOMETHING if we are blessed enough to discover what it is and are willing to work just as hard to refine it. We all need help. That's what teachers do. They make superstars --- some are just not as famous as others.

· · · · ·

During my career, there were numerous times when, often unexpectedly, teens became "mentally fragile" --- not so much "unstable," but in desperate need of care and attention. Some (thankfully) recovered fully. Others (sadly) sometimes went completely off the rails. The most effective therapy was ridiculously simple --- required only two key body parts --- ears and shoulders.

· · · · ·

As a parent, I have seen the evidence of the fantastic success of my former charges --- photos, graduations, careers, promotions, etc. Just curious, but I'd love to hear their thoughts about how two people, they and their spouse, raised multiple kids in the same household, and for years of applying essentially the same rules, got such diverse results. Give that one some thought, and they might discover why educators get addicted to educating.

· · · · ·

Before firefighters, emergency medical technicians, and police officers, parents and educators were, and still are, the first responders.

· · · · ·

Between the pandemic and the "gundemic," teachers have had to first endure a punch in the gut and then a kick in the teeth. More than ever, they are feeling expendable --- disposable --- and rightfully so. Education, never the best-paying of professional careers, is the ultimate labor of love. Circumstances being what they are, it's easy to understand why there is a growing shortage of teachers, and the situation is growing increasingly desperate. If you have not noticed, you soon will. That phrase, "a good education," is beginning to take on a whole new meaning.

· · · · ·

I have no desire whatsoever to return to the classroom, but I sure would like the opportunity, just for a moment, mind you, to crawl inside their little heads to see what makes them tick--- these fascinating young people that you all are raising these days.

· · · · ·

Can you remember some of the thoughts that routinely ran through your little head, and those of your friends, as high schoolers sitting in your typical class? Now, compare YOUR thoughts from then with the thoughts of typical high schoolers now. WHOA!

· · · · ·

I have 2 granddaughters. One is 11, and the other, 16. Both play in their respective school's orchestras --- the older, viola, the younger, violin. I recently attended their annual spring concerts. In my (unbiased) "granddaddy opinion," they were both wonderful --- fantastic --- but I was also struck by the DIVERSITY within each group --- tall ones, short ones, black ones, white ones, brown ones --- but all that mattered was the MUSIC they played together --- TOGETHER --- so beautifully. Their teachers, conductors, must work awfully hard and care an awful lot. It's sad that we assign each other to teams according to demographics.

• • • • •

Smarter than they thought, stronger than they thought, BETTER than they thought --- the best thing about teaching and coaching is being able to place glasses on the faces of young people so they can more clearly realize their own greatness. I've got a list.

• • • • •

Participation in sports is a good idea because you can apply lessons from COMPETITION in ANY venue.

• • • • •

I had an exchange student once from the beautiful island nation of Malta (in the Mediterranean). I recently posted a question to educators, current and former, and asked them how they are coping with schools, guns, and all that goes with them. Not surprisingly, our fame has even spread abroad. This was that former student's statement: "I still can't understand how your teachers in America have to deal with 'what if' there's a mass shooting. It's baffling . . . and very sad." I will share 3 of the responses I got from current educators (there were more):

1.   "Unless you've been in a classroom, you have no idea what we do beyond our basic job description. It is those things that are stressful. We are tired, but we do what we do for our kids."

2.   "I was just telling Lucas (husband) that during lockdown drills some students would try to sit between me and the door so I'd have to tell them to move. They would say that they would protect me, but I had to explain that it would hurt me more if they were injured, and like any other situation, they were my kids. The thought of both wanting to protect and others wanting to protect me, even in drills, was overwhelming. The bond between teachers and students can be so strong. I cannot imagine the emotions during and after when it's not a drill."

3.   "The last few days have been heart-wrenching, to say the least. I spent my last 8 years (of 40) in the classroom with 18 lively 4-year-olds. Among many goals, I wanted to foster a love of school. After all, this was their first

experience. My biggest dread was gathering them into a small bathroom together with lights out and door locked and keeping them quiet. With only my flashlight on for light, these kids were amazing. Not a peep! I still tear up at the thought of the trust they had in me. I pray none of them ever have to experience such a thing."

You can draw your own conclusions.

· · · · ·

I once saw on television a man who had terrible difficulty with both verbal, as well as physical, skills. However, after being flown (by helicopter) over the skyline of a major city, it just happened to be Paris, could stand in front of a very long canvas, and draw a giant replica of that entire skyline with incredible, amazingly detailed accuracy. That's when I first researched the term "savant." He has done so with many of the most famous city skylines of the world: New York, London, Berlin, and others. I recently witnessed a performance by a world-renowned pianist, unusually short in stature, totally blind and seemingly "afflicted" with a malady that severely affected muscle control in his arms and hands. Words like breathtaking, and marvelous immediately came to mind, as his huge audience, thoroughly mesmerized throughout, watched as he became one with those 88 keys! I once saw a swimmer in the Special Olympics who had no arms (from elbows down), and no legs (from knees down). I could only imagine the looks, laughs, he must have gotten when he first told people he wanted to be a SWIMMER. He had to be "placed" onto the starting blocks, and at the gun, would simply "fall" into the water and begin "paddling" furiously, and obviously, quite effectively. Then there was the gymnast, Special Olympics again, whose floor exercise was as strong and graceful as any you could imagine. He had amazing upper body strength and control, but had no lower body at all, waist down. Each of these remarkable human beings, in a variety of classifications, was considered "disabled." Surely you have seen a few. I find them incredibly inspiring, and possibly worthy of a new and different classification --- ENabled --- for their awesome ability to "refocus" others. They can totally change a mindset. I think I now know why my responses were disbelief, insult, and even anger when any of my former charges, student or athlete, with no such "classification", approached me, head hung, and dared say, "I can't."

. . . . .

I sat and had a light brunch with an "old" friend today. This is Carly. Before she graduated from high school, she was a very good assistant to my chiropractor --- dependable, knowledgeable, and hardworking. That was seven years ago. She has since married, graduated from college (UNC Wilmington), and just finished her first year as a teacher in an area high school. Maybe you can tell by her smile, maybe not, but Carly has that magical combination of "tough and loving" --- an especially valuable gift, especially these days, especially in high school. She loves it - comes up with original, creative little projects for her kids. Her reputation has begun. They love her. She'll be Teacher of the Year one of these days. We hadn't spoken in person for a long while, and she decided to reach out to me a few days ago. We agreed to meet at a local Panera's to chat for a while. She told me about a special, favorite kid in one of her classes. She told him she knew what he was doing, but never complained too loudly about how often he came to class reeking of marijuana. She'd respectfully confront him, and he'd just smile. In the end, she was happy that he was coming to class at all. Carly was there for his graduation a couple of weeks ago. She was so proud of him, and she told him so. She knew he would need that diploma to better provide for his tiny daughter. Carly had reached out because she needed to tell me Tavon was shot and killed a few days ago --- no known killer, no known motive. She was heartbroken and just needed a shoulder for a while. Carly has "those" eyes. You've been there, haven't you? I reminded her how much it can cost to care, and ironically, the price rises with the depth of caring. She already knew. We exchanged vitamin words for 2 hours, and she looked stronger when we said goodbye. She'll be okay. It's easy to cheer for young people like her.

· · · · ·

When you think about it, time and again, TEACHERS are almost always among the first, first responders.

· · · · ·

There are schools out there where a visit to the principal's office is not necessarily a "bad" thing --- and that's a GOOD thing.

· · · · ·

Veteran high school educators remember hugging former charges at their graduation ceremonies and having their caps fall off.

· · · · ·

There are bonds that develop between coaches and athletes that last a lifetime and can bring real tears, even after decades of absence from each other. They become very real fathers and mothers, sons and daughters and are deeply loved as such. Sports? YES!

· · · · ·

When teachers/coaches retire, the one thing that always makes them smile --- brings them the greatest joy --- is realizing the number of great PARENTS they helped raise.

· · · · ·

Dogs and teachers have a lot in common. Some call them "man's best friend;" others are reminded that their name, spelled backward, also carries profound meaning. They sometimes become loyal, dedicated members of the family, and perform genuine miracles daily, routinely going beyond the call of duty to protect those they serve, even readily sacrificing their own lives in that service. They patiently tolerate little ones tugging on their ears, but even the tiniest ones will demonstrate surprising ferocity if the lives of those they love are endangered in any way. They are, at once, the ultimate GIVERS and FORgivers. They don't really ask much, and rarely hold grudges. It's hard to imagine a world without them.

· · · · ·

Teacher/coaching friends, wouldn't it be the greatest thing to stand out on some large field and have each young person you ever taught or coached, in one long line, and one by one:

1. Stand directly in front of you and introduce themselves,

2. Tell you the year(s) you taught or coached them,

3. In a sentence, share how you positively affected their lives,

4. Give you a big hug?

No matter how long it might take, even if it means standing in the rain, you'd patiently give each their turn and be deeply grateful for the wonder-filled opportunity --- SIGNIFICANCE. Now just try to put a price tag on that!

. . . . .

It's no secret that great teachers love to teach, and the main motivation --- the most rewarding aspect --- is THE KIDS. Every year, teachers adopt a whole bunch of them, intentionally or not, and they keep those kids with them, in their hearts, for the rest of their days. One of the most precious bonuses of it all comes when those kids raise their own great kids. That simply HAS to be the greatest reward, except their becoming wonderful GRANDPARENTS too! When they proudly display those precious family photos, I always try to add a "heart" emoji.

. . . . .

We have all heard of lawmakers, peacemakers, troublemakers, and a few othermakers, but to that list, LEADERMAKERS should be added. You've met them. They are quite common in the military, business, sports --- people we respect, revere --- even cherish. It's impossible to be a true leader maker without a well-developed, almost uncanny ability to LOVE, from compassionately to toughly.

One principal who hired me some years ago is just such an individual --- truly one of a kind. Many others apparently thought so too. Among other prestigious titles held and awards won, she was the President of the Virginia Association of Secondary School Principals , and oddly enough, she grew up an only child. She once told me, "You don't work FOR me, Jerry; you work WITH me." That one line guaranteed my undying loyalty. I cannot count the number of high-octane leaders she has helped develop, however, I will introduce you to one of them. Not long ago, she was tapped to head a very special high school in San Diego (nationally, the 7th largest school district). Another wonder-filled product of our leaders maker --- exceptionally gifted in her own right --- she has obviously impressed the top brass in her district --- witty, intelligent, dedicated, and incredibly caring. A veteran school administrator, she confesses that this latest assignment will be, like the several others she has mastered, quite the challenge. Approximately 1,500 students,100% Black and Latino, the task is indeed daunting --- students running the entire gamut from gifted to gangbanger. Yet, I cannot think of a better candidate to fill the position. She has met every task with skill and grace while raising three amazing daughters (the oldest, a recent graduate of UCLA). Her stage --- high schools --- is a tough performance ANYWHERE, but again, I cannot think of a finer general to lead this latest war. Today, I had the special privilege --- the joy --- of sitting and having lunch with these two amazing human beings --- the general and the captain. It was easy to see what they both had in common. They have that rare capacity to LOVE young people deeply and more persistently than few others) I have ever seen. They will always stretch for that extra yard. It wasn't the first time I've told them how much I cherish them, and it's not likely to be the last.

· · · · ·

Think about it --- Columbine, Virginia Tech, Sandy Hook, Marjorie Stoneman Douglas, Uvalde, and recently, Newport News, there are many others. In each case, "regular old teachers" either risked or sacrificed their lives to safeguard their young charges. Are we really paying attention?

· · · · ·

Kudos to all the kids I ever taught, coached, or mentored in some way --- those of you who have become INCREDIBLE PARENTS, GRANDPARENTS, or fantastic mentors yourselves! Facebook has helped me track your many amazing accomplishments in the most difficult and important arena of them all! YOU HAVE DONE SO WELL! Senor, Mr. G., Coach, G-Man couldn't be more PROUD! Is it okay to say, "keep 'em comin'?"

· · · · ·

When I was a teacher and coach, I remember the many faces of my charges. Back then, they were just kids themselves --- couldn't imagine themselves being called "dad" or "mom." Now, so many of them are, quite literally, the parents of thousands. (I've seen the photos.) They have done well and contributed much in the ubiquitous struggle against evil in this world. It is a most humbling thing to have been blessed to witness that.

• • • • •

Think of any service-oriented career you like: medical professional, minister, counselor, therapist, PARENT? --- whatever --- and chances are, sooner or later, a true COACH will be called upon to play that role.

• • • • •

Years ago, when I was a classroom teacher, I'd do a little demonstration. Before the class began, I would reach into my pocket and pull out a gold coin (no, not on a teacher's salary) and place it on the floor near the door. Then I would invite a volunteer to come to the front of the class and stand on the side of the room opposite the door. Instructions: "If you can pick up that gold coin, it's yours, BUT there is one small condition. You may not move your feet." Everyone in the room could see this was impossible, so I'd have that student to be seated. The gold coin represented their goals (gold) in life. More often than not, young people get fixated on their goals and forget they must "move their feet" in order to achieve them. Moving their feet meant regular attendance, good study habits, good work ethic, and included all the other usual virtues of life; trustworthiness, respect, determination, etc. Moving their feet, barring any unforeseen circumstances, would virtually guarantee they would eventually get to the point where all they'd need to do is bend over, pick up their gold coin, put it in their pocket, and walk out the door. Young people need to be reminded to stay focused on the tasks at hand --- the responsibilities of today --- and to tackle tomorrow's challenges tomorrow. They will usually experience greater success (and happiness) along their journey too --- one step at a time.

· · · · ·

Sadly, nearly every veteran teacher and coach has seen it. Their classroom or practice venue unexpectedly becomes "something else" --- a haven, a sanctuary, a refuge --- where kids will do anything to keep from having to go home.

· · · · ·

Want to know one of the most priceless lessons educators learn from teaching? They learn that rich kids and poor kids, every race and nationality, given the opportunity, can all perform admirably on any stage. Because rich kids normally have access to more and better resources, they usually appear to be able to "excel" in greater numbers, but in truth, the skill levels (including intellectual) are otherwise quite equal. It is a most satisfying, gratifying realization, and plays a huge role in those powerful motivations that drive teachers to give so much, often for meager material reward. But then, that's probably why someone came up with that quote about goals not being about "incomes" but "outcomes."

· · · · ·

It takes a great deal of FAITH to be a farmer. There is unpredictability in the seeds they plant, the soil in which they plant them, and of course, there's the weather --- drought, flood, frost, wind. Still, every day, they work long hours planting with the full expectation of a bountiful harvest --- their bounty ultimately feeding thousands. Exhausted at day's end, and with calloused hands, they smile and present their produce to a hungry world. In many ways, TEACHERS are a lot like farmers. (Pardon me. I am still trying to find comfort.)

· · · · ·

When I consider the definition of "addiction," my initial reaction is concern --- sadness --- but then, I realize TEACHERS and COACHES fit that description too, and I feel better.

· · · · ·

Too many people, for too long, most of them with no clue about what actually goes on in our schools, have been bashing teachers, accusing them of "brainwashing" kids, when the most severe "brainwashing" likely occurs at their work, around the water fountain, or in their den (in front of the television).

· · · · ·

Veteran educators are among the world's best "people readers." They tend to be very good observers of WHAT people do, but they can be truly gifted when it comes to discerning WHY people do what they do --- masters of the M & M Principle: Method & Motive. Some have skills that can border on the supernatural. It follows that, if someone wants to know what a human being is all about, simply poll a number of trained, experienced educators --- those who have mastered those critical skills: assessment, performance, outcomes --- LEARNING. And interestingly, the age of their charges has little to no effect on the accuracy of their observations, or the conclusions they draw from them. If people-skills are so important, then educators (among others admittedly) have traditionally been woefully undervalued and underpaid. But then, for most of them, money was never among their main motivations anyway.

．．．．．

Magic happens the moment teachers and coaches convince their young charges they have magical powers that no one else ever knew were there --- best drug ever.

．．．．．

Tommy, Melissa, Robert, Denita, Colin, Ronnda, Timmy, Jereliz, Emmett, Pete --- a few (of many) students I taught or coached who all had ONE thing in common. I was WARNED by parents, other teachers, older siblings, neighbors to beware of them --- that they were "difficult to handle," "trouble(makers)." "do-nothings," and "losers." Know what else they all had in common? They all became some of the most AMAZING human beings I ever had the joy to know! Like everyone, they had their struggles, but they turned out to be incredible when it came to meeting and overcoming life challenges. Today, they are successful and significant --- happy in their careers, families, and lives --- beaming. One is my financial advisor! I couldn't be more proud, impressed, humbled, grateful --- BLESSED --- to have them in my life. In the end, THEY taught ME a critical (two-fold) lesson: 1. Always get to know people for yourself. 2. Never underestimate the potential of young people. In life, everybody wants to be the teacher, but it's better, best --- wonderful --- to be the STUDENT!

· · · · ·

There are likely more retired educators around these days than you know. Some have managed to last 'til full retirement. Others, for a variety of reasons, decided earlier that a career change was best for them. (Sadly, there are now more of those than ever.) It's not hard to understand why. You already know teachers don't choose that career for the money. (Most, in fact, would actually consider that notion laughable.) In the messages that I've posted from teachers recently, there appears to be one purpose they all have in common. They want to make a difference in things, and they are willing to do whatever it takes to do so --- a heavy responsibility these days, but still a burden that nearly all of them are willing to take on. Especially recently, they've been beaten up, then beaten down. Those who care about this country may want to stop and think about that. I can't quote the data regarding education in other nations, but I can say with confidence that we still have some of the finest in the world. Few people have ever ventured into those trenches, but there are still many who profess to know all that goes on in the classroom and how to "fix" it. In how many workplaces can any citizen, on any given day, show up without an appointment and dictate to college-educated professionals how to do their job? I am only one voice, and I am certainly no prophet, but for many of those professionals, the pilot lights are slowly dimming, and too many more have already been extinguished.

· · · · ·

Some years ago, there was a unique student at the high school where I worked. She had been a bit of a "party girl," and had actually dropped out the year before I was assigned there. I quickly discovered she had not quite finished her party girl ways, so I'd find her sitting outside my office on more than one occasion. Before you judge, in our talks, I discovered she was ABSOLUTELY BRILLIANT, and until she graduated from college (valedictorian), had no idea who she was. She did know that she wanted to change the world. Today, she is very happily married, has two fine sons, and is one of the finest, most dedicated teachers I've ever known. In a recent post, I asked how teachers were dealing with the recent school shooting in Texas. This was her response: "It's hard. It's a hard reminder that I would give my life for my students that I love and treat as my own. It's hard to think about what those teachers went through. It's hard to think that after all I do, give and sacrifice for my job that I could lose my life. It's soul crushing hard to think about. I scan the recess areas and always have a plan for my students. Whether it's the right one or not I hope and pray to never find out. That's tiring. I practice lock-down drills with tears just wanting to leak out, but I stay calm and fearless for my kids. It's exhausting to watch over 20 kids always wanting them to be safe, happy, kind, hardworking, and well educated. It's mentally draining. I'm tired. I'm hurt. I'm just sad." In so many of these terrible school shootings, THIS is consistently who teachers have been --- demonstrating this exact attitude. I've been blessed to know so many. Heroes all, they have been willing to sacrifice their lives for their --- OUR --- kids. NO price is too high.

. . . . .

You can offer people prescription glasses, but you can't make them wear them. A teacher's job is not to teach, but to offer opportunities to learn.

. . . . .

The subject matter is not as important as the ability to "read" their charges --- to discern countless, subtle differences in body language and vocal tones is crucial to their success in the classroom. (Of course, this is especially true of teens and pre-teens.) Experience counts. The best educators, by necessity, are amazing in that regard, making it a double tragedy when one decides to leave the profession "prematurely."

. . . . .

Once upon a time, "heroism" to a teacher meant helping young people to graduate and be successful in life. Nowadays, sadly, the meaning has changed. They must be medal-winning warriors and literal lifesavers --- classroom/warzone. Combat duty pay anyone?

· · · · ·

The following is a message I received today from another of my former champions. Many of them had no idea how much they "fueled me" --- not with gas or diesel. This stuff is NUCLEAR! "You know, your words would mean the world to me any time, but in light of the obvious distress and palpable pain in your posts of late, your words are priceless. I don't pretend to be without biases, but I think most of mine are fairly objective. For instance, I know I have a very low threshold for stupidity and incompetence...but I recognize the difference between those who choose to behave stupidly and those who are uninformed or otherwise incapable of discerning the intellectual wheat from the chaff. The first, I will tolerate. The second, I will go to great lengths to guide or lead as necessary. I'm pretty sure I learned that from YOU. I'm also pretty sure it wasn't part of the Spanish curriculum, but it has certainly been one of the most important things anybody ever taught anyone. I can't imagine what it must feel like to be you, knowing that you have single handedly reached down into the very souls of countless students you taught, athletes you coached, and just plain lucky people who crossed your path and touched them indelibly and often immeasurably. You will never know how many you have caused to get their s*** together or maybe literally talked them off the ledge, but that score is being recorded elsewhere. I'm pretty sure there is a comfy cloud waiting for you to park your weary self one day...just don't be in a hurry to go check it out. Promise? As for your daughter marrying an Air Force dude, well, I guess I'll have to give you a pass on that one (her sons --- Naval Academy). I'm sure that must be his only shortcoming if he is good enough to marry a Gaines girl!" These are better than money.

· · · · ·

Much has been made of the term "legacy." Just how much better off is the world for you having been a part of it for a few minutes? Arguably, the best representation of the term lies in the quality of the OFFSPRING you help bring into this world. If you have done a great job of that, then no one can ever call you worthless. You can feel happy and confident that you made a significant, positive contribution to a world that will forever need it, for those kids' lives will leave indelible marks upon the lives of countless others. THAT is the truest definition of WEALTH. That is LEGACY in its purest sense. As an educator/coach, I was blessed to witness so many of my charges become the most magnificent, wonder-filled examples of great parenting. When I think about it, the numbers are staggering, and that gives this old-timer all the hope in the world. I KNOW what a combined contribution those young people will make in this world, many are already well into the game, and I am humbled to have touched, just for a moment or two, the lives of those who have done such a magnificent job in one of the toughest careers imaginable. This, then, is a small tribute to each and every one of you. You already know who you are. How can you not? Be patient; the cavalry is on the way.

· · · · ·

The greatest gift of the greatest teachers lies in their ability to uncover hidden gifts of those who had no idea about the depth of their own greatness. And it is a gift unto themselves as well.

· · · · ·

Yesterday was an extraordinary day, not because we had a wonderful dinner at some fancy restaurant, or because I caught a citation fish. Yesterday, I was visited by a former student --- one of my best ever. She had brought her husband, and two of her three sons along. The third, married to a girl from Spain, lives in Germany. Her last name was TEW. I gave each student a Spanish name, so naturally, I called her "DOS." To this day, she describes herself as an "introvert" --- never talked much in class. We shared one of those special "eye-to-eye" relationships in class. We could read each other perfectly. She phoned ahead (not surprisingly) to let me know when she was close, they live near Raleigh, NC, so I was watching when they pulled into my driveway. They had decided to come up for a quick weekend vacation in VA Beach. I ran out of my front door as she jumped out of their car. Just like in the movies, we ran across my front yard to greet each other. Nothing was said, we just fell into each other's arms and held on tight for a long while as if to make that moment last forever. Jay, her husband, was smiling ear to ear. I whispered in her ear just how happy I was to see her, and after a while, we pulled away and looked at each other --- wet cheeks and red eyes said it all. Her two sons (college-age --- NC State) naturally didn't seem particularly thrilled to be visiting their mom's old high school Spanish teacher, but before long, we were all laughing and chatting in my living room. Jay is originally from the Boston area. They met in college (VA Tech), and each is truly brilliant. Dos then paid me the ultimate compliment. She said I had told her the most valuable thing she ever heard as a teenager. She still remembered that I once told her it was okay to be herself --- to be "different" --- that she needed no one's permission. (She teared up a bit on that one.) Dos is fifty-one years old now, with little hints of gray around the temples of her thick head of curly red hair. As you might guess, our goodbye hug was deeply moving --- longer and even legendary, with no words necessary. I was sooo happy, still am. As they pulled away, I thought to myself, "I'll just bound back across the yard and leap up onto my front porch, as I used to do once upon a time, then my knees, and back and...well... EVERY PART said, quite clearly, "are you out of your ever-lovin' mind?" I WALKED back into the house. I was still smiling though!

. . . . .

Teachers and coaches are addicts. They get high on the performances of their charges, and they can never get enough. It is what they do. They realize EVERY young person is gifted in some way, and if --- IF --- they can be there --- present --- when the light goes on, when those young ones discover themselves, there is no greater drug. In truth, EVERY person in EVERY field of endeavor should be so addicted --- a teacher and a coach. That is especially true of every PARENT. In all likelihood, you already know quite a few Hall of Famers. Do you --- can you --- include yourself? If so, then do so --- PROUDLY. It's okay.

. . . . .

If teachers teach long enough, sooner or later, they will run across a family of GENIUS KIDS, and their parents often have no idea how they got that way.

· · · · ·

Finally got to sit down to lunch with those old educator friends I told you about. It was everything I thought it would be. The four of us (dare I say it?) total nearly 160 years in education! The conversation, as you might imagine, was lively and non-stop; the memories ---many and priceless. It was wonderful. The hugs when we met were long --- genuine, and when we left, even more so. Just before we were done, I reached into my jacket pocket and poured a handful of wild cherry lifesavers onto the center of the table. With big smiles, each of them happily, almost eagerly, shared them. It was a perfect finish to a very sweet occasion.

· · · · ·

In nature, rainforests cleanse the atmosphere we breathe. They play a huge role in the formation of clouds that, as their name implies, bring rain. Their leaves are miracle workers. We hardly notice their dried remains when they flutter to the ground. Their purpose fulfilled, we rake and bag and burn them in the fall. Fortunately, a fresh new crop, in due time, replaces them. Next week, a few old friends and I plan to meet for lunch --- mostly just to share memories. Old teachers do that from time to time to remind each other that their lives/careers truly meant something. Sometimes they forget. Retired now, these old warriors were absolutely spectacular educators. There are still more out there clearing the air than most people realize. I was blessed to meet my share of them. Who can know the impact they had on this world --- the collective caring they showered upon the heads of who-knows-how-many young seedlings? Like strong trees, they stood, spreading branches that shaded countless saplings until they, too, rose and took their place in the sun. The conversations will be priceless, but no words will be necessary. Still days away, I am already excited. I will bring all my ears.

· · · · ·

Educators get a sense of genuine need when they step into a classroom and look into the eyes of their charges.

· · · · ·

Speaking to maybe 100 staff members at a local hospital recently --- caregivers --- I again looked into eyes that reflected similar, almost desperate, needs --- affirmation, encouragement, compassion, appreciation.

· · · · ·

Watching a World War II documentary the other day, I learned that roughly half the native population of the island of Okinawa died in a terrible conflict that they had absolutely nothing to do with. I thought of the Holocaust, and slavery, and Israel, and Gaza, and Ukraine. Then, I thought of how often, in the throes of agony and hopelessness, the innocent actually welcome --- pray for --- the relief of death. To know one's history is essential. We must learn and never forget.

· · · · ·

Ironically, what all great educators do best is STUDY! They create great relationships by noting the finest details in the lives of those who sit in front of them each day.

· · · · ·

Of all the inspiring messages you can take from this year's Olympic games, one stands out above all others. Pick the sport/venue --- CHAMPIONS KNOW HOW TO FINISH! Nobody can argue that!

· · · · ·

People can be gifted in any number of ways, but to have had the opportunity to PARTICIPATE in some (any) sport at some (any) level is a gift in itself. That's why we respect the game.

· · · · ·

Did you ever consider how many races, religions, states, and nationalities are represented on a U.S. Olympic TEAM?

One gold medalist this year is from Homer, Alaska (of all places). They send this message every Olympic year --- the most genuine, effective international ambassadors ever --- and we still don't get it.

· · · · ·

If the Olympic Games were a skyscraper, there would never be a top floor.

· · · · ·

"The thrill of victory" is not an emotion exclusively reserved for athletes.

· · · · ·

Some of you (Oldtimers) will remember the old TV show, "The Wide World of Sports," hosted by Jim McKay. Part of the intro included the phrase (with video), "...the thrill of victory; and the agony of defeat." If you have ever trained hard and then competed hard, you will know how deeply the second part of that phrase influences the first. No matter the competition, athletes (many Olympians) often cry when they fail to reach their goals. However, sometimes years later, you might see them again --- more formidable, indomitable. Continue to get back up. It's always worth it.

· · · · ·

Perhaps more than anything, great educators teach their charges to scrutinize --- to make closer, more accurate assessments of their own identities.

. . . . .

Some of the most fantasmagorical young people that I've ever met somehow blossomed in the midst of some of the most horrific home environments. Parents didn't make them, nor did teachers, coaches, counselors, or any mentors. They were just.............. THEY are the "true riches" of this (or any other) nation.

. . . . .

JMHO (again): There may be countless, priceless experiences in this life, but there is nothing --- NOTHING --- quite like raising a great child who becomes an even greater adult.

. . . . .

I could describe my career of dealing with teens in a gozillion ways, but BORING certainly wouldn't be one of 'em!

. . . . .

Great teachers and coaches love meeting young people who were told they'd never amount to anything.

· · · · ·

A small minority of athletes "make it big" --- NBA, NFL, MLB, PGA, etc. --- but something interesting happens to many who do. Suddenly, they have more money than they can spend in three lifetimes. For some, there's an understandable, irresistible "urge to splurge" --- buying everything they could ever want. Then, they realize something. Fortune and fame are fleeting. Much of what it took for them to make the professional ranks in the first place --- work ethic, discipline, honesty, gamesmanship, and even forgiveness (INTANGIBLES)--- often feed/fuel a sincere desire to HELP OTHERS. They start foundations, create scholarships --- donate to charities. Perhaps more than anything, sports teach you to be "otherly."

· · · · ·

All these years later, I am just now realizing how much (as their teacher/coach) I LOVED my kids. Every chance I get, I tell them (some, now in their 60's). (Very) veteran teachers and coaches know this feeling well.

· · · · ·

As a coach, I never allowed my athletes to say, "I can't." In my life, I have seen too many athletes do so much more (with fewer gifts) than what the naysayers were certain was

impossible. Watch the Special Olympics (or Paralympics --
- any sport). It has to be one of the most INSPIRING things
anyone could ever witness.

· · · · ·

JMHO: So, one of the largest school districts in the land
plans to prohibit cell phones in classrooms. Teachers all
over the country could have told you it would come to this.
Now, the Surgeon General is confirming the accuracy of
those teachers' "prophetic utterings," Especially since the
epidemic, educators everywhere have been taking a
merciless, undeserved beating from many who had no idea
--- likely, a huge reason why teachers (in frightening
numbers) have been leaving the classroom (that price to be
paid later). Think about how many devices that little gadget
has ultimately replaced --- even your television! As wonder-
filled as they are, there just MIGHT be something to the
many, detrimental effects those little devices can have on
adults, let alone kids. ANY teacher/educator could have told
(warned) you. In fact, they probably did.

· · · · ·

One of the most important lessons in competition is that
YOUR OPPONENT IS NOT YOUR ENEMY. In fact, your
competitors are indispensable when it comes to YOUR
personal growth. You must never hate those crouched next

to you on the starting line, standing in the other dugout, those on the other side of the field/court, or those in the office down the hall. Instead, try to match (surpass) their intensity. It is only the LOSING that you are free to hate. But even then, it is up to you to make it only a "temporary setback." Such an attitude adds sincerity/significance to post-game rituals --- handshakes/fist bumps, smiles, and the well-worn, "GOOD GAME!" Rightly played, everyone wins!

· · · · ·

There is a huge difference between having a gift and choosing to be determined enough to maximize it.

· · · · ·

Ever thought about how much athletes invest in their pursuit of greatness? Consider anyone --- little leaguer to Olympian. When their day is done, and they "hang up their cleats" at long last, their accomplishments (no matter how amazing) are inevitably surpassed --- forgotten. Some attempt to "preserve their glory" by building shrines to themselves --- display cases, walls, entire rooms --- highlighting their hardware --- ribbons, medals, trophies, plaques. (I'm guilty too.) Competitors often fear being forgotten. But as athletes grow old, their trophy worship gets old too. Even the hardest fought-for ones get relegated to old shoe boxes and desk drawers. In time, trophies tarnish and fall apart anyway, and many come to realize the true reward for all their efforts lies in strong bonds --- RELATIONSHIPS --- forged through time, drops of blood, and gallons of sweat. In time, true competitors realize (and are grateful for) other fellow athletes, be they teammates or the "opposition." Those trophies don't rust.

· · · · ·

As we grow from childhood to adulthood, the chapters of our lives come and go quickly. There are names and faces that your mind associates with those chapters --- key individuals that leave a lasting impression. There might be long periods between contacts, but the friendships --- the memories --- last a lifetime.

· · · · ·

I had great friends on my college track team, but from the start, Nick and I grew particularly close. We were both hurdlers --- trained, raced, sweated, and hurt together. We had a great coach who pushed us hard, but Nick --- a couple of years older than me --- pushed me like no other. I can hear his voice to this day, urging me along --- "C'mon, Gaines, let's get it." I was a rookie, but he quickly made me feel like I belonged. No indoor facilities or rubberized tracks back then, we'd pound the asphalt on some days, and the concrete on others --- side-by-side during long, tough, training sessions until we got it right --- "smoother than a baby's behind," as they say. When practice was over, we'd sometimes have to hold each other up as we'd stagger back to the locker room, pausing occasionally when one of us would suffer one of those excruciating bouts of "whole body" cramps --- indescribable (they simply have to be experienced). I learned early on the meaning (and the rewards) of HARD WORK.

· · · · ·

I had lunch with Nick today. We reminisced about old times, of course. We were five hurdlers once; now we are three. I enjoy talking --- listening to --- my friend. He has traveled the world, visited more than sixty different countries on five different continents, and is one of the most intelligent human beings I have ever met. His greatest quality, though, is his HEART. I mean that both ways --- the fiercest of competitors, and one of the most compassionate of human beings (to all living things --- even trees). Before the usual farewells, we saved the world a dozen times and vowed to continue to contribute to the cause of humanity in every way we can. (The goodbyes are more serious now, you know.) The "man hugs" are sincere --- reassuring. He always whispers, "love ya, Man," but what I always hear is, "C'mon, Gaines, let's get it!"

· · · · ·

It is DEEPLY HUMBLING and GRATIFYING to think about how many great kids my great kids have raised --- my own, my former students, my former athletes --- especially when I consider the collective blessing they are sure to be in this troubled world. Some of my great kids have raised great kids who are raising great kids --- not "old" --- EXPERIENCED! Thanks in a huge way to GREAT PARENTS! It's okay to be PROUD --- even to brag a little!

· · · · ·

IMMIGRATION is such a huge issue these days --- a complex problem that comes with its own set of challenges. However, there is also a MIGRATION occurring that is at least as complex, and potentially even more hazardous. TEACHERS today are abandoning their classrooms at an alarming rate. People acknowledge the importance of educators, but in recent years, teachers have experienced an unprecedented level of persecution that is driving them (in alarming numbers) from the profession — the STUDENTS and the COMMUNITIES --- they love and serve. The disappearance of that one "love component" from any society, and everyone eventually suffers. In this case, it is especially true --- "You don't miss the water until the well runs dry."

ENCOURAGEMENT

Word Hugs

All my life, I kept these thoughts to myself, thinking everybody would think I was, at best, weird, or at worst, totally insane.

· · · · ·

You hear the names almost every day, crack, meth, opioids, and the potent new demon on the block, fentanyl. Once upon a time, the list was far shorter --- most, in fact, were quite beneficial. When they migrated from the hospital to the street, they changed everything --- mind, body, and yes, soul. It's sad; we must be reminded of the most potent drug ever --- ENCOURAGEMENT. Too many, too often --- too early --- simply lose their CHEERLEADERS.

· · · · ·

"They said I'd never amount to anything." This can be a huge discourager to some, and a powerful motivator to others. So much depends on the audience, doesn't it?

· · · · ·

Have you ever seen a "totally worthless" human being? Is there any such thing? In the majority of cases, it's more a matter of WILL (won't) than worth.

. . . . .

My cousins and I often laugh about growing up poor. On a recent visit, one of them, a special favorite, spoke about a New Year's "celebration" she once had at her house with her adult kids. She had left the house on a quick errand, and when she returned, her kids were celebrating with a cheap bottle of champagne and a jar of pickle relish --- wonderful memories.

. . . . .

Some special people can drink with their minds. It, too, is intoxicating, and perfectly legal at any age.

. . . . .

Every world record holder is proof positive that "impossible" really isn't. Don't be intimidated; be INSPIRED!

. . . . .

There are thousands of ways to excel. We all have them. The key lies in finding one (or more) that can diminish the thousands of ways to hurt.

· · · · ·

Some people look at others' great achievements ---
athletes, entertainers, businesspeople --- and are
DISCOURAGED. They think, "I could never do that" (hence,
all the hero worship). Instead, they should be INSPIRED.
They SHOULD think, "I bet I can do that too! In fact, I think
I can do that --- even BETTER!" The most successful people
have discovered something --- hard work is the best-
disguised blessing in the world.

· · · · ·

If you look closely, you'll see there's really no such thing
as ordinary people, yet, those are usually the ones who most
appreciate ordinary things.

· · · · ·

You ever talked to a person and their conversation felt
like a hug?

· · · · ·

It IS possible to change the way things are. You CAN
make a difference in things.

· · · · ·

The differences between what you WANT and what you NEED parallel the differences between SUCCESS and SIGNIFICANCE.

. . . . .

We will always know just enough to leave enough doubt to make FAITH an absolute requirement.

. . . . .

Those new photos from the James Webb telescope have you thinking, don't they? Trying to wrap your mind around all that space, all those unfathomable distances, aren't you? Then, there's that "time" factor. It's enough to make you feel rather insignificant. Those pictures probably have you asking yourself "those" 3 questions again (the ones you'd just as soon forget):

1. Who am I?

2. Where did I come from?

3. Why am I here?

. . . . .

By comparison, our entire planet is a speck of dust. For that matter, what is our entire solar system compared to all that? And what difference can YOU make? In the whole scheme of things, no matter how long you live, you either choose to love or you don't. That simply HAS to be where the significance lies. What else could possibly matter? Besides, it answers all 3 questions.

• • • • •

One of the greatest "mind-levelers" is TRAVEL. There's a good reason for that. Better than anything, travel offers EXPOSURE to other cultures --- people, foods, ways of thinking. Travel teaches us that diversity is actually a GOOD thing, and often teaches against that most ancient religion, "Holier Than Thou." Travel teaches that, by default, isolation simply propagates ignorance. We sing, "God Bless America (and He has --- greatly), but it may not have been the greatest blessing that, geographically, our country lies exactly between two gigantic oceans.

• • • • •

Heaping praise upon the proud is like inviting a starving person to a smorgasbord. They elbow their way to the front and make repeated trips to the table. They use a tray instead of a plate. Heap praise upon the modest, and they take a few choice portions, but only after waiting patiently to allow others to go ahead of them. You've seen this.

• • • • •

I used to wonder what thoughts went through the minds of truly world-class athletes when they had to face me in a competition, especially when I was just a young upstart. I tried my best to make sure they didn't feel like the adult lion swatting a cub. Only once in my career did I ever defeat one of them --- Olympic gold medalist and former world record-holder, Bob Beamon. (I must admit he had a very rare "off" day.) Still, that day, I only managed silver. My job was to make sure that, no matter their credentials, I was willing to strap on my gloves and go toe-to-toe with them, however briefly. My greatest claim to fame, if I even have one, is that in all the various track events in which I participated (maybe 8 or so), I never once won with my personal best performance. Don't be intimidated by "champions;" use THEM to bring out the best in YOU! Even the tiniest cubs have claws.

· · · · ·

Sometimes, life unexpectedly puts a footprint in your freshly poured, perfectly finished concrete. It causes you a little more work --- a little more stress --- but remember you've already proven yourself handy with a trowel. That's how you got the job in the first place.

· · · · ·

It takes a lot of hard work to become successful, but it is what we DO with that success that reveals the ultimate goal, sought by all of us --- SIGNIFICANCE.

. . . . .

Many choose ignorance because it dulls their sense of responsibility. "Knowing" prompts them to "do something." It's no coincidence that, at the root of ignorance, is "ignore."

. . . . .

There is something I feel I must say here. So many friends are eager to praise these words of mine. I rush to tell you that they are NOT MINE! I cannot take credit for them. They are thoughts that unpredictably come into my now-graying head, and I think they are inspired by a Love that is not my own --- a Love that touches you --- moves you --- deeply because, like the rest of the world, we all CRAVE it. In my own power, I could NEVER move people in such a profound way, but know this: On any given day, I do NOTHING that any one of YOU could not. Just think, "If you had enough pennies, you could purchase all of Manhattan."

. . . . .

We call it a number of things, you know a few, but don't you just love the "stuff" that rises up in the hearts of little-known competitors that makes them believe that, YES, I can take down this opponent, even if that opponent is already a proven legend?

. . . . .

Many people try to make life trouble-free, makes perfect sense, but in doing so, they may actually be creating additional ones. Since troubles are inevitable, they will face disappointment, frustration, and possibly even rage. The last one bringing with it a whole bevy of potentially dire consequences. Instead of trying to eliminate troubles, we're better off learning how to deal with them . Otherwise, they become stumbling blocks to progress that can utterly destroy potential.

. . . . .

More pats on the back usually translate to fewer pats on the bottom.

. . . . .

Champions GIVE you nothing! If you wish to win against them, you must TAKE it. They know if they perform at their BEST and fail, there will be disappointment, but no shame. They can look you in the eye, shake your hand, and you will know their message, "I'll be back."

. . . . .

Some years ago, I lost my father to cancer --- not long after that, my brother. In recent decades, so many have had to endure that dark, scary journey --- family and friends hoping against hope for the same miracle outcome while not knowing, in the end, who will be among the chosen. We've lost a lot of beautiful human beings --- some of the finest. Still, at any given moment, everybody knows somebody, or somebody who knows somebody, who is in the midst of a battle for their very lives. Life comes with more than its share of worries and concerns. It certainly would be nice if we could once and for all be totally rid of this hated scourge.

. . . . .

A former student-athlete reached out to me today for advice, one of my greatest joys. Her middle school son is a marvelous athlete and makes straight A's. Visibly upset, he woke her this morning in tears to tell her he had forgotten an assignment --- that was some of the best, most joyous advice I ever gave.

. . . . .

"We want you to be successful," they said --- "Go out and make something of yourself" --- more, bigger, better. They rarely tell you the best way to do that is to choose significance over success by building OTHERS --- more, bigger, better.

. . . . .

The birds, the insects, the creatures of the seas --- the mountains and the trees --- are NOT LIKE US, and yet, there is much to learn from them all.

. . . . .

We are generously afforded the challenges of exhaustion, but never the luxuries of quitting.

. . . . .

Music, nature, or just a few quiet moments can be great therapy. Life WILL demand that you slow down and occasionally spread the wings of your mind --- visit a couple of those places prepared just for you. Words are rarely, if ever, necessary.

. . . . .

The better job you do raising your kids, the more it hurts to see them leave. They go out into the world and, despite all your misgivings, demonstrate how well they learned those lessons you so skillfully, patiently, and diligently taught them. It's okay; your reward --- the pain-killer, though none are TOTALLY effective, takes form in that sense of pride and fulfillment you feel as you watch them fly on their own. Nothing says SIGNIFICANCE like leaving a quality LEGACY. Educators can relate!

. . . . .

It may come at a variety of different stages, but we reach a huge turning point in life when we can look at ourselves and say, "I need to work on me."

. . . . .

Anyone can observe "METHODS" --- WHAT people do --- but it is more valuable (and more difficult) to discern "MOTIVES" --- WHY people do what they do. The "M & M Principle"!

. . . . .

You shouldn't rush through life, but you SHOULD be aggressive in your search to find joy in it. The only genuine, lasting joy lies in the relationships and memories you generate during YOUR time here. The only downside is that joy, if and when you find it, always tends to accelerate the years. Ask any senior citizen.

. . . . .

Life's simple pleasures are the best. Have some!

Though both are desirable traits, STRENGTH is one thing; STAMINA, quite another.

· · · · ·

It takes PEOPLE to inspire PEOPLE. Only PEOPLE can raise life's aspirations from successful to significant, so that should be everyone's ultimate goal. Those whose life goals run contrary to that can only cause strife, division --- turmoil. They are a ready and perpetual challenge --- competition. They must be defeated, overcome --- conquered at all cost if humanity is to grow and thrive as it must surely have been originally intended.

· · · · ·

You can start by making up your mind that, for the next 24 hours, you will not LOSE YOUR COOL with anyone --- family members, friends, acquaintances, co-workers --- total strangers. Then, expand that 24 hours to 48, 72 and so on. In time, make up your mind that, for 24 hours, you will BE KIND to everyone --- family members, friends, acquaintances, co-workers --- total strangers. Then, expand that 24 hours to 48, 72 and so on. Part one makes part two easiER, but not necessarily easY. That's where your CHARACTER comes in.

· · · · ·

They say the job is too big, so they decide to do nothing.

· · · · ·

How many can look into a mirror and honestly see what's actually there? Self-delusion runs rampant.

· · · · ·

The battlefields of STUDENTS have always been many and varied. It takes a special level of discernment, skill, and caring to fight alongside them: parents, educators, counselors, ministers, and so many others. In the end, a win for them is a win for the world.

· · · · ·

Think about the different aspects of GROWTH --- physical, mental, emotional/spiritual. Now, think about how INTERDEPENDENT they are in the development of "proper" human beings.

· · · · ·

Feeling Down, Disappointed, Distressed, Distraught? Don't Dare quit; you're not Done! Until time reveals truth, nobody wins and everybody suffers.

· · · · ·

It is wise to become an ENCOURAGER. In so doing, you can help heal wounded hearts while making good ones even better. This includes your own.

· · · · ·

Everybody's hurting and needs a hug, but the comforters are all busy with other things. When we cease to care as we should about others and focus only on ourselves, there is no better formula for the ruin of a people, a nation --- a world.

· · · · ·

We should learn not to curse the storms and the darkness. That's where the heroes and champions are forged.

· · · · ·

Validity, veracity, integrity, honesty --- a beautiful recipe, but add just a pinch of DOUBT, and not only is the flavor of the dish destroyed, but its nutritional value as well.

· · · · ·

If you refuse to be broken, then you cannot be fixed.

· · · · ·

Peaceful, calm, cooperative, caring, sharing, merciful, forgiving, friendly, respectful, honorable, truthful, loyal OR belligerent, anxious, uncooperative, indifferent, greedy, callous, begrudging, confrontational, disrespectful, cold-hearted, deceitful. Now I ask you, why in the world would anyone CHOOSE the latter list when the first is, obviously, so much better, beneficial, and less stressful for everyone involved? We are an odd lot, aren't we?

· · · · ·

Looking back, one of the greatest things to ever happen in my life was that no one in my immediate orbit ever had it easy. Struggle is truly a backdoor blessing.

· · · · ·

If no one is perfect, then everyone makes mistakes. If everyone realizes everyone makes mistakes, then there are basically only two responses: stubborn disregard (pride), or genuine repentance (humility). Both require CHANGE, but there is a price to pay for each --- how heavy the price depends on us. One is far worse than the other. It impedes growth, eradicates learning, and can only, ultimately lead to destruction. Still, amazingly, that one remains our preference.

· · · · ·

How can I convince them how great they are and how much they can accomplish unless I challenge them to do things they never thought they could?

$\cdot \ \cdot \ \cdot \ \cdot \ \cdot$

A lot of home runs and knockouts have been scored simply because someone kept swinging.

$\cdot \ \cdot \ \cdot \ \cdot \ \cdot$

It is not enough to simply discover your gifts and share them with the world. Your ultimate purpose cannot be fulfilled until you decide to aid others in the discovery and development of their own. This is life at its fullest.

$\cdot \ \cdot \ \cdot \ \cdot \ \cdot$

Have you ever really given serious thought to the power of "fear?" Its opposite --- "FAITH" --- must be equally strong to effectively counter (conquer) it.

$\cdot \ \cdot \ \cdot \ \cdot \ \cdot$

You do all you can, as often as you can, in every aspect of your life. You grow and learn it's best to consistently set "high bars" for yourself --- character, integrity, responsibility, dependability --- the whole nine, but you learn early on that, being human, you cannot perfect even one of them. Your job is simply to watch and learn as much about as much as you can. This is how you grow properly, for this is how you endow yourself with a good and generous --- precious --- heart. It is the ultimate life gift you present to yourself. Your life goal then becomes to share the lessons you learn with those you meet along the way --- those who need to know. There will be many, but here will forever be those (sometimes with less than half your experience) who will insist they know more/better. You mustn't worry; they are there for other instructors. YOUTH carries with it many blessings, but an overdose of PRIDE is never one of them. HUMILITY, instead, is the underrated gift --- the key ingredient in the recipe for all good, generous --- precious --- HEARTS.

. . . . .

Everybody wants their lives to count for something. You have to hurry, but you can't rush.

. . . . .

A silly little thing, perhaps, but I have always been amazed at just how fast direct sunlight can melt away the heaviest frost on a windshield.

. . . . .

Integrity, especially these days, requires healthy doses of courage and character.

• • • • •

Many events go into the chapters that form the novel that becomes the story of your life. When your one-of-a-kind book is closed, an entire library is archived in the minds of those who knew you. Cherish every life; make great memories.

• • • • •

Ever see a child get hurt, stumble around, arms outstretched, blinded by tears, while bumping into things, and desperately seeking to be comforted? That happens throughout life.

• • • • •

You can live a mistake-free life if you learn a LESSON from every poor decision.

• • • • •

Silence sure speaks loudly sometimes, doesn't it?

• • • • •

Elvis Preslcy, Elizabeth Taylor, Whitney Houston, Michael Jackson, Princess Diana, Prince, Walter Payton, Muhammad Ali, Robin Williams, Gary Coleman, Heath Ledger, John McCain --- just to name a few. Most likely, you have during your lifetime witnessed the passing of many famous people --- individuals whose careers you followed, true superstars you may even have idolized through the peak (and sometimes the decline) of their respective careers. You may even have some autographed piece of memorabilia from one or more of them --- perhaps an item for which some might offer a tidy sum. Yet, with all their wealth and fame, in death, not a single one of them is, in any way, better than --- superior to --- YOU.

· · · · ·

John Wesley says it best --- "DO: all the good you can, by all the means you can, in all the ways you can, in all the places you can, at all the times you can, to all the people you can, as long as ever you can." In so doing, you may not become as "famous," but you will surely be as important --- as precious --- as anyone. Do good!

· · · · ·

Think of the people you know --- any and all demographics: race, nationality, religion, profession --- and if you're honest, you realize the vast majority of them are wonderful, kind --- normal --- human beings. It's interesting (sad?) how just a few "bad apples", present in EVERY group, can move some people to label them ALL as "bad apples." We are broken; can we ever even be fixed?

· · · · ·

These are tough times; almost everyone is struggling. One of the best cures in the world is to go out and HELP somebody else in some way. With so many out there, it won't be hard to find "legitimate targets."

· · · · ·

All of us did silly things when we were young --- when PRIDE, in one of its many forms, ruled in our decision-making. The "wisdom of the years" comes cloaked in an "attitude of HUMILITY" --- strength in disguise.

· · · · ·

As kids, we are "carefree." Yet as adults, we allow ourselves to be crushed by worry --- things over which we have little to no control: politics, the environment --- squabbles of every description (worldwide). Have you ever been under water 'til your lungs felt like they were about to burst? Then, you explode to the surface and take that first, deep breath! Remember how that felt? It's time to come up for air --- be a kid again --- if only for a breath or two.

· · · · ·

In life, I've found that if you care deeply enough for long enough, your reward, in time, will be WISDOM.

· · · · ·

Some will call you a dreamer --- maybe even lazy because you like spending time in your personal, quiet spaces --- a bench, or a stump, at the water's edge --- fresh or salt. Places with lots of trees, especially old-growth forests, are nice. Some prefer "vistas" --- mountains and valleys and such, especially in the fall. Of course, there's the traditional favorite, the porch swing, but quiet spaces are for people of ALL ages. The world today can be a nosey ...er... noisy place. "Retreat" means different things to different people. Is that why they call them "refuges?" Hopefully, yours are convenient --- easily accessible. Get away from all the loudness, and REplace it with songbirds and all those peaceful sounds that water makes --- just for a while. Quiet spaces help you sleep better.

· · · · ·

A simple, four-word compliment that's not heard nearly enough: "I KNOW YOU UNDERSTAND" --- so therapeutic for both sides.

· · · · ·

People call them "obsessive," "compulsive," "picky," "particular," or a host of other things, but some of the world's finest people in their respective fields are "sticklers" about those proverbial "little things."

· · · · ·

If allowed, children, not really knowing what's good for them, would dine exclusively on sweets. Freedom plays the same role in adults. Instead of freeing themselves to do whatever they want, they should free themselves to do as they should. They know the difference.

· · · · ·

Just how many different roles do you play each day? How many hats do you wear? You must sometimes match the attitude with the outfit, coat and tie or formal dress, when the "real" you...well. Other times, a cheery voice and a smile may cleverly disguise genuine frustration (anger?) at, say, a rude cashier. You can think of others. It's hard playing "let's pretend" so much, but it's more routine than most of us realize. It SOUNDS good when people say, "get real," but most times, it's probably not a good idea.

· · · · ·

Bad things in life are viewed as punishments by some, and tests by others.

· · · · ·

A wise, old teenager once told me, "I can't trust me because I don't know who I am yet."

• • • • •

Many are they who are quick to tell you, without telling you, that your opinions, your experience --- your interpretations --- mean little. They say, "Let me tell you what to do --- how to think." Life has taught YOU lessons too.

• • • • •

It's a good idea to remind each other often that we are all mortal.

• • • • •

Looking back, it's easy to see that our lives get divided into chapters --- periods of time that vary in length and run the gamut from terrible to amazing. What we make of each chapter may vary greatly, but there is something to gain --- something to learn --- from each. Mistakes are not as lasting --- not as damaging --- if we make LESSONS of them. Among those lessons is a most critical one --- how we come to value OTHERS --- ALL others.

• • • • •

This thought has likely crossed your mind on more occasions than you're willing to admit. How many decisions, big and small, have you made that, had you not made them, or maybe "tweaked" them (even a little), would have changed your life entirely --- EVERYTHING?

. . . . .

In a very real sense, sharing thoughts and messages, on just about any subject, "frees" me. It's good to find the keys to your prison.

. . . . .

Human beings have the ability to change the environment to suit their needs. Not unique really, as beavers, to a limited extent, can do the same thing. One thing, however, remains constant. Consider any age --- any time in history --- and you'll discover the things that mattered most then, continue to matter most to this day. Think about that.

. . . . .

Liberty is a wonderful concept, but we have become so enamored --- so intoxicated --- with it that it has become our idol. We even have a statue to prove it. We have begun to worship freedom instead of the Giver of it. In so doing, we are "freeing ourselves to death."

• • • • •

So often in life you hear people say, "It's not all about you," but when you think about it, it really is.

• • • • •

When you plant seeds of ENCOURAGEMENT, you will reap a bountiful harvest, however, unlike other farmers, you cannot schedule when. Encourage anyway.

• • • • •

How many "BUSINESS PEOPLE" do you routinely deal with, often by necessity --- sales, repair, healthcare, insurance, legal, etc.? In your dealings, HONESTY and INTEGRITY are, understandably, highly desired, but sad to say, rarely expected. In fact, we too often EXPECT to be mistreated --- even ripped off, especially certain categories of clientele: seniors, women, poor. It's such a relief , joy, to deal with businesses that value those precious business attributes. It's nice when they value your satisfaction over the same old "green motivations" too.

• • • • •

There's a lot to say about the meaning of life. Above all else, everybody simply wants to be somebody, but ideas on how to go about it vary quite a lot. Being somebody doesn't mean being rich (though many would argue that). People just want to know that their life means something. Isn't that the real goal of every school --- every classroom? No matter the subject, teachers must first convince students that they make a difference --- that their unique skillset matters. Destroy, or even distort, that one, key item, and their personhood goes with it. Isn't that why drugs and alcohol are so dangerous --- so destructive? It is critical to learn the difference between success and significance. When people think of "success," they usually think of "things." When they think of "significance," they usually think of "OTHERS." Humans have forever been obsessed with accumulating more and more "stuff", only to realize later THAT view of success is an empty bucket, but most realize it too late. It's a fine goal to want to BE somebody, but if that goal is to be done well, it usually means being somebody TO and FOR somebody else.

· · · · ·

If you truly believe they are precious, then the last thing you should want to do is waste time and life. We must find ways to make our time on earth count for something positive. Choose your own; there are all sorts of options.

· · · · ·

You mustn't be afraid to be "that one" who stands up and shows the world a different way of looking at things --- of doing whatever it is that you are gifted to do. You may be called weird; you may be called crazy, but there has never been, nor will there ever be, another quite like YOU. The world is sometimes skeptical, often downright fearful, of new ideas and unique perspectives.

· · · · ·

As amazing as human beings can be, so much that they touch eventually ends up contaminated.

· · · · ·

You must choose your bat carefully --- the right length, weight, and thickness --- before stepping up to the plate. Get as comfortable as you can --- thankful for that extra practice. The pitcher is very good, or so you've heard --- intimidating standing out there glaring directly at you, expressionless, and drooling like some dog eyeing a bone. He's got quite the repertoire of pitches, or so you've heard. His fastball is deceptive --- his "out pitch." He sometimes throws AT batters --- tries to "back them off the plate," or so you've heard. They say he's hit a few --- beaned a couple, ruined careers. Lefty, righty, switch hitter--- it doesn't matter to him. YOU must be ready, find a way, make good contact --- get around those bases. YOU must score! It's not easy ---

never is. It's a great help to have a dugout full of teammates. They must be good too. Only --- ONLY --- together do you win.

. . . . .

LIFE is a lot like a baseball game.

. . . . .

A few years ago, I watched an interview between a sportscaster and Russel Wilson, the quarterback for the Seattle Seahawks. When asked about who motivated him most, Wilson related a conversation he had with his father (just prior to his Dad's death). Russell had shared with his dad that coaches repeatedly told him he was too short and did not have the arm strength to play in the NFL. His father's advice: "SOMEBODY'S gonna do it, Russ. Why not you?" Today, Russell wears a Super Bowl ring.

. . . . .

Last year, we watched a freshman quarterback enter the biggest game, not only of his young life, but the biggest game in college football --- The National Championship! He calmly led his team, the Alabama Crimson Tide, to an absolutely amazing come-from-behind victory over an incredibly talented Georgia Bulldog team. Tua Tagovailoa left onlookers scratching their collective heads (after screaming them off). Immediately after the game, he ran into the stands to find his father. They embraced for a long while. He went on to say his dad meant everything to him, and he acknowledged his faith in Jesus Christ as his family's faith appears to be quite strong. I hear he has a younger brother who is at least as good. Venus --- Serena?

· · · · ·

In a very similar scenario on Saturday --- a local gridiron contest pitted "David & Goliath" against each other. The entire sports world was convinced David was going to receive another drubbing, as was the case the year before. But again, a young, untested walk-on confidently trotted onto the field and led Old Dominion University to a stunning upset of then thirteen-ranked Virginia Tech. I remember Blake LaRussa's dad ALWAYS being his biggest fan. Blake did not have anywhere near the size of the typical college quarterback. No offense, but he still looks pretty scrawny to me, but like Russell Wilson, what he lacks in size, he obviously makes up for in skill and moxie. I did not have to hear him say it even once, but on more than one occasion, he has probably asked, "Why NOT you, Blake?" Moms are indispensable in any society, of course, but great dads...well...it's obvious that young people kinda need them too. Twenty-five years from now (I'll likely be long gone), when Blake's kids attend ODU, I think they should each receive a full scholarship.

. . . . .

As a child, I remember reaching up and tugging on the broken handle of our refrigerator door. Looking inside, I remember seeing only the gallon-sized glass jar of cold water --- nothing else --- and being unfazed by the rust that formed inside the metal cap. It always smelled like pickles. There was NOTHING else in there --- not even the lingering aroma of last night's leftovers. There were never any. Dragging over a kitchen chair, I remember climbing up to look inside the freezer only to find thick, frosty-white ice totally covering the interior (some will remember). That caked-on ice made it nearly impossible to remove the only item inside --- an ice tray (some will remember). Those are priceless memories. Some among you will remember, and wouldn't trade them for the world. Tough times can be powerful, back-door blessings.

. . . . .

A lot of people, especially in recent years, have given Christianity a bad name. Truth be known, I can understand why non-Christians look, as they do, at those who profess to be. Based on LOVING --- a VERB more than a noun --- you can easily confirm (verify) people's true belief system by what they DO. Just watch. These are very trying times (as EVERYBODY knows). Often, I find myself running around not knowing up from down --- who to help first (while blood is spurting from ME too)! People find their comfort in many, many ways. Please feel free to choose as you wish. This one is my own, personal choice, and for me, in every way, it has proven the best.

· · · · ·

Among their many skills, people are wonderfully adept at pretending to be something they're not --- they bend truths to fit their needs at the moment and have no qualms whatsoever about creating a football bat if it serves their purposes.

· · · · ·

Christianity has suffered a series of black eyes recently --- so many wolves in "cheap" clothing. Despite all the deception, personally, Christianity answers nearly all of my most profound questions about life. If done right, there are so many different ideas, it is the way I've chosen to live.

· · · · ·

Like you, I stared in awe at those spectacular photos from the Webb telescope. They only confirmed what I had already concluded. In MY mind, the odds of this universe coming together by chance are remote. "Some unfathomable entity HAD to have organized it," I concluded. Then, naturally, I considered what possible significance MY meager existence might play in the midst of all of it. If heaven does exist, and I believe it does, it doesn't matter whether I call it Paradise, Nirvana --- Valhalla --- MY ticket will have only ONE name on it. It won't matter if my father was a great leader, or my brother, the worst murderer in history. My acceptance qualifications depend wholly and solely upon me and how I spent MY time here. According to the rules, the God I serve believes that too, but no matter what religion, race, nationality --- god ---everybody would do well to prioritize that one aspect of life. In fact, that should be everyone's primary focus. What have I done? (And humility is a good thing.) If my ultimate goal is to please myself by pleasing others, then my motivations are really the best kind of selfish.

· · · · ·

So I play the game to the best of my ability --- according to those rules I've learned, rules I didn't write. While everyone around me makes their own choices, mine are just that --- my own. That is how I make sense of it all (in case you ever wondered).

· · · · ·

Another long chat with yet another former charge. We sat on a bench, at opposite ends, of course, under a tree with a marvelous view of a local river bordering the Norfolk skyline. She, too, "just wanted to talk" --- to bring me up to date with what's going on in her life. After two children, she also found herself divorced a few years ago. She seemed almost amazed they couldn't make it work --- "irreconcilable differences, like they say in Hollywood," she told me. It was amicable enough, and she was finding it intriguing to get back into the dating scene at age 50. She invited her son to help her do some painting at home to see what he thought of that. He's 17, so you can guess some of the stuff he said. She is one of the strongest (mentally and physically) people I've ever met, yet she is extremely sensitive. On at least four occasions, there were tears as she reflected on happier times. She was always brilliant (bragged a bit, in fact, about how easily she made "A's" in my class). Yet, here she was, making it, but very much in need of a vitamin pill. Fortunately, I had a few. I remember her smile as she walked off to her car --- that old familiar bounce in her stride.

· · · · ·

You've witnessed sad times where people you know have lost someone dear, no details necessary. Watching, listening, you quietly shared their pain --- suffered alongside them. Convinced they couldn't go on --- pain so deep it could never possibly heal, you became their much-needed, much-appreciated shoulder. (You've been there yourself.) Don't you find it amazing, that once they emerge on the far side, they appear so much stronger? The deeper the hurt --- the greater the loss --- the bigger the difference. They go from deeply hurt to miraculously healed. It's the strangest thing. They develop greater insights, wisdom, patience --- POWER --- seemingly from the very one no longer with them. You've experienced this, haven't you? It's not at all uncommon.

· · · · ·

You know, most of us are born into this world, and almost as soon as we can talk, we start wishing our limited years away. The statements (and thoughts) usually begin with, "I can't wait 'til..." Next thing you know, much of your lifetime has passed, and you're listening to your own kids say the same thing.

· · · · ·

Just a suggestion: At the end of every day, just before you lie down to rest, think, it helps if you have a mirror, "What SIGNIFICANT thing have I done today?" More often than not, the answer will involve something that you did for someone else. You may want to "chew on" that one for a while.

・ ・ ・ ・ ・

With LEADERSHIP, policy, viewpoint --- agenda --- can be debated, arbitrated --- compromised. With CHARACTER, honesty, integrity --- righteousness --- leave no room for flexibility. In all things RELATIONAL, choose wisely, and always be keenly aware of the CONSEQUENCES of choice.

・ ・ ・ ・ ・

Through all your struggles, there comes a time when you know you're going to make it. Be encouraged; you're still here.

・ ・ ・ ・ ・

Of all the gestures in body language, arguably the most telling is a lowered head.

・ ・ ・ ・ ・

It's often hard to do the right thing, but it's always the right thing to do.

・ ・ ・ ・ ・

I often contemplate what might have been before accepting what's meant to be.

• • • • •

In sports (football, baseball, track and field, tennis, golf, and others), athletes are asked to compete in increasingly more challenging levels: trials, quarter-finals, semi-finals --- FINALS. Many never consider the fact that competitors must be at their BEST when they are most battered --- bruised and exhausted --- having fought their way through tough practices and tougher opponents --- essential if one wishes to be called CHAMPION. That's why sports are so loved by so many. More than anything, they teach us LIFE.

• • • • •

Everybody loves a winner --- fierce competitors who come at their opponents with everything they have: Brady, Tiger, Biles, Djokovich, Phelps, and Curry (to name a few). Their opponents fear them because winners constantly remind them of that old Yogi Berra quote, "It ain't over 'til it's over."

• • • • •

We do not write the script of our lives. Time will teach you what a great idea it is that you don't.

• • • • •

Adam and Eve received simple, clear instructions as to how to behave, in their case, what fruit NOT to eat. Whether you believe the story or not, one truth remains clear --- undeniable. Nearly ALL the wrongs that human beings commit, they do so KNOWINGLY. We are naturally, incurably, rebellious. War, crime, racism --- all types of cruelty --- are a manifestation of what must lie within us all. We are infected, and the infection makes REPENTANCE and FORGIVENESS absolutely essential if we dare dream of PEACE.

· · · · ·

Everyone wants to be healthy. Athletes ultimately train to better "communicate" with their bodies. The better conditioned they are, the more detailed, accurate --- beneficial --- the interactions. The human body, for example, has several ways of letting you know when you eat something you shouldn't. It will not only try to "dissuade" you from eating that particular thing again but will also penalize you when you don't listen. The message: if you LOVE yourself, you will COMMUNICATE and LISTEN, or PAY THE PRICE. Think about that. The exact same message is being sent to all humanity. We must not be listening.

· · · · ·

The older you get, the more you appreciate opening your eyes each morning. Family, friends, dawns, and sunsets are wonder-filled bonuses.

· · · · ·

It's usually desirable to perfect certain skills but learning to cope well with the loss of loved ones is an exception. After all, those most skilled --- most experienced --- are the very ones who have suffered most. You've been there --- just a thought.

· · · · ·

Startling revelations have been realized through the simple act of sitting and staring out of a window.

· · · · ·

Paradise lies in little things.

· · · · ·

We are only given one life, but if we live it properly, one life is enough.

· · · · ·

A former athlete of mine once asked, "Hey, Coach, just how good were you when you were competing?" My response: "I ran just fast enough --- (long) jumped just far enough --- to be insignificant in elite competition."

· · · · ·

In sports, as in life, if you are too scared to fight, you are probably too weak to win.

· · · · ·

It's not surprising that people are negatively influenced by negative environments, but isn't it amazing how some who experience crushing poverty and terrible cruelty grow to be some of the most generous and loving?

· · · · ·

I don't believe I have ever met a single human being who was not, in one way or another, truly GIFTED. Most don't realize this, and sadly, many never find their own, special gifts. But if I CAN, in some way, help them discover that gift, that is how I CAN best better the world; that is how I CAN find meaning --- significance --- in this life, so I CAN best qualify to live in the next. The greatest gift of all CAN be me!

· · · · ·

Humans have always insisted on taking the Instruction Manual out of the hands of the One who wrote it. They repeatedly misinterpret it, and sometimes write their own -

-- endless laws and proclamations, worshiping their intelligence while destroying wisdom --- the clay advising the Sculptor. They convince themselves they are the best interpreters/teachers/leaders, and sometimes even declare themselves divine. Hope remains a distant dream.

· · · · ·

Life is a race. Though you may, at times, have to pick up the pace, it's best not to make it a sprint. Sometimes, conditions are difficult --- hot, cold, windy, muddy --- but they are just tests --- challenges that everyone, at some point, must endure. Ideally, they strengthen, inspire, and fuel confidence. Sometimes, you pass other runners. The struggles are real, and occasionally some take a spill. You might take their hand, help them to their feet, run alongside for a while, or ignore them altogether. That's where you learn the power --- the mutual blessing --- of encouragement. You should notice the (changing) scenery. Simple things like leaves, streams, and creatures can ease the cramps in your legs (and mind), soothe the burning in your lungs, and give you a second wind. Along your route, some fans cheer; some jeer (or throw things), but you cannot --- dare not --- quit. It's all part of your race. With all its unforeseen peaks and valleys, it is always best to continue east. That's where the sun always rises.

· · · · ·

Open a window --- a simple act, a powerful act.

. . . . .

In an amazing variety of ways, tears are good.

. . . . .

Sometimes I apologize for the length of a particularly long post. I must confess that my apologies are not sincere. I am convinced it's GOOD to read more.

. . . . .

Heard someone speak this truth today: "Pardons are more about MERCY than they are about POWER."

. . . . .

As a little boy, You are rarely in such a hurry that ten seconds will make that much of a difference. I, too, daydreamed about visiting faraway places. Back then, I rarely left the state --- never saw a mountain or a waterfall. Today, I can't count the awe-inspiring places across the globe my eyes have beheld. Many of you know those feelings. I hope you realize the BLESSING.

. . . . .

Beautiful weather, rainy, sunny, snowy, the giggle of a child, a warm pot of soup, a visit and a hug from a dear friend, the smells of spring, the aromas of Thanksgiving and Christmas, dazzling sunrises or sunsets, quiet solitude, baby toes. "These are a few of my favorite things." Care to add one of your own?

· · · · ·

Just as the word "believe" implies doubt, the word "faith" implies assurance. We can believe in some, and we can have faith in others.

· · · · ·

They say courage is not the absence of fear, but the will to overcome it. A "me first" attitude, no matter how it is expressed, is nothing more than a demonstration of FEAR. To do what is GOOD and RIGHT requires introducing FAITH into the equation --- the expectation that our actions will (surely) bring about positive outcomes --- and that can work wonders.

· · · · ·

While everyone is replaceable, we should live our lives as if they represent unreachable goals for anyone to match.

· · · · ·

You have probably beheld some of the world's most awe-inspiring, natural wonders: mountains, waters, lands, forests, flora, fauna --- the heavens. You've probably wondered about all that went into the formation/creation of such places --- all in this little, blue speck spinning around in the unfathomably huge vastness of the universe. You have probably wondered about HUMANITY --- the ones who have the ability, albeit limited, to reshape and manipulate it all. And you have wondered...

· · · · ·

If you have been blessed in some way in this life, as most of us have, doesn't that mean that God must think something of you? And if He does, why should it matter to you what others think?

· · · · ·

It is interesting how, especially in politics, characters are so adept at "turning things around" --- accusing opponents of the very traits and tactics of which THEY are guilty. Growing up at the height of the Jim Crow era, accusing fingers pointed at ME from all directions --- ugly, dirty, unintelligent. I had to adopt, then teach, the same goal --- "turn things around."

· · · · ·

Through the years (there have been a few), many have wondered and asked what it was like being a "first." In my case, it was being the first Black scholarship athlete at Virginia Tech. Only now do I feel prepared to share my "blackground" about that. Upon arrival there, I discovered some students did not want me on "their" campus, but there were more who did, and welcomed me. I discovered some professors did not want me in "their" classrooms, but there were more who did, and welcomed me. I even discovered some teammates did not want me on "their" team, but there were more who did, and welcomed me. I discovered that, no matter what anyone thought of me, I still had to go out and perform in "their" grand stadiums against some of the best athletes in the world. I discovered that, nearly everywhere I went, some did not want me on "their" turf --- military, career workplaces, grocery store --- but there were more who did, and welcomed me. I discovered the "whys" behind the saying, "It is what it is." I learned the world is the world and it's not likely to change any time soon. Like everyone else, I had one life to live, and despite all the naysayers, I had to be at my best in every venue. I was far from perfect in any one of them. In time, I learned EVERYONE is a "first." Even the life journey of identical twins is not "identical." What mattered most was how I chose to respond to the world's inevitable, and many, critics. Being a first taught me there's a tremendous amount of FREEDOM in optimism and faith, and with that liberating realization came a heightened, wonder-filled sense of SIGNIFICANCE and PEACE.

· · · · ·

Life can make the heart grow bigger, but the greater the growth, the higher the price that must be paid for it.

· · · · ·

Even if there is absolutely no one around, people who hook a big fish WILL talk (mostly to the fish itself)!

· · · · ·

Once upon a time, I used to be an athlete (and Chicago used to be a cow pasture). At the peak of my "athletic prowess," I realized that no matter how hard I worked, I still marveled at just how much BETTER other athletes could get. Sometimes they were just more gifted; sometimes, they simply worked harder; sometimes, both. Almost imperceptibly, athletes learn that the human body is an incredibly complex combination of bona fide miracles, not only with its PHYSICAL capabilities but also with its MENTAL and even EMOTIONAL gifts. Older now (much), I better understand how, with all its complexities, the human body can also have countless maladies --- things that "just go wrong" --- with any and all of its convoluted, intricate workings. Ultimately, I learned the "truly great ones" arrive at a vital realization. When it comes to true "athletic prowess," at the end of every aspiration (and it's spelled in many ways) is COMPASSION.

. . . . .

It is no coincidence that those who were once criticized, persecuted, abused, beat down (and up) are often the most merciful, generous, compassionate --- VICTORIOUS!

. . . . .

What an amazing gift --- the heart that beats inside your chest. No wonder it is so often used to symbolize life. You get to choose how to use it --- to discover its incredible potential (or not).

. . . . .

Have you watched a toddler react to seeing himself in a mirror for the first time? With time, mirrors send a grand variety of different messages. If the messages are read properly, those images can be highly educational.

. . . . .

Faith is not about mystical powers. It's more like confidence on steroids.

. . . . .

"Hearing" is the simple, sensory function of the ears. "Listening" however requires engaging the BRAIN, and more often than not, the HEART.

. . . . .

A "THREEFER": If you make no attempt to fill your days with good deeds, you will eventually curse the passage of time.

. . . . .

For those who seek greatness, hard training is not a matter of "punishing" your body (and mind). Instead, it is a TEST. Only those who dare to push the limits reap the rewards.

. . . . .

Youth is just a special type of ignorance. Because it affects us all, everyone eventually --- desperately --- needs true Jedi Masters to help lead them out of that darkness. That's why a lightsaber is the only weapon a true Jedi really needs.

. . . . .

It is impossible to serve well, motive is key, without eventually garnering sincere praise for having done so.

. . . . .

Human emotions are at once peculiar and spectacular. But few can match those you feel when you help those who (perhaps for a lifetime) have been told they are worthless, realize they are, in fact, PRICELESS.

• • • • •

Think about how many roles you play each day. There are usually more than you realize. Being human, no one plays any one of them perfectly. You play "let's pretend" a bit in some, but overall, you score better than average in most. Even in best-case scenarios, life can be complex. Don't be too quick to beat yourself up.

• • • • •

Despite appearances, there are a lot of absolutely amazing people out there, so don't be discouraged. One of the things they most have in common is they don't usually make a lot of noise, but it's uncanny how they show up just when you need them. Keep your head up. Those others...well...you can't help knowing the deal with them, can you? In the end, they need you even more.

• • • • •

PRAISEWORTHY. If ever there was a true "therapy" word...

RACISM

Prejudices = Pre-judge-us

In a world of dogs, imagine being hated for being born a cat.

. . . . .

It's often not as much a matter of what we DON'T see as much as it is a matter of what we WON'T see.

. . . . .

Being the FIRST Black athlete at Va. Tech, for a while, also meant being the ONLY black athlete there. Naturally, I stuck out like that proverbial "sore thumb." I had never known such loneliness. In no time, however, I discovered something interesting --- something deeper, more complex, perhaps even sinister. Having been raised in the South, and having personally experienced segregation and Jim Crow, my exposure to white people had been (understandably) limited. I was quite familiar with the "N"- word, but at the same time, I never realized there was an "N-word" for Italians, Polish people, Latinos, and Jews too. In my innocence --- ignorance --- these had always been "just other white people." So my education would ultimately include a mandatory, heightened awareness that there are (many) people in this world who work hard to "elevate" themselves above others for incredibly superficial reasons --- history, culture, freckles (???) --- denigrating those they perceive as "different" or somehow "less than." Inadvertently, these same people taught me one of life's most precious lessons. Through them, I learned to truly treasure DIVERSITY in all its many forms --- all kinds of people from all kinds of places and all kinds of cultures. I was able to maintain the hope that those famous phrases I read about (and recited daily in elementary school) might one day mean what they claimed --- "liberty and justice for all," "that all men are created equal," "inalienable rights." I wouldn't wish my hardships on anyone (though many others suffered far worse), but in retrospect, at least for me, those lessons proved invaluable.

· · · · ·

How many problems in this world are caused by people who want to force others to think --- believe --- as THEY do?

· · · · ·

Who DIDN'T learn about George Washington's "I can't tell a lie" story, cherry tree and all? Conversely, who DIDN'T learn about the very real black women who were the "hidden figures" of movie fame? Which is more relevant? Some need to really rethink CRT.

· · · · ·

At some point in your life, you may have been moved to contemplate an old query, "What's it all for?" I am a Black man --- hardly any news. Most of America cannot understand what that means or how that must feel, especially during the era that has included my lifetime. I know that, when I look at myself in a mirror, or when I look around me, it's not a recent revelation, I am sometimes, I will say this now, brought to tears at what life has so routinely demanded, even when we've done everything "right." It is encouraging that so many now see though. The war has begun in earnest, and yes, there ARE very legitimate concerns, mixed in with my very sincere hopes. These are, indeed, interesting times in which to be living.

· · · · ·

Another black perspective: Superstar athletes and other entertainers have forever garnered most of the attention, but the lives of the Bernard Shaws, Mae Jemisons, Neil deGrasse Tysons, and Colin Powells of the world quietly touch us just as profoundly. They dared to swim in those unknown waters too and surfaced triumphant on the other side. The courage and determination it took in those arenas must have been at least as tough as those on the gridiron, the court --- the stage. After decades of being told what you're not --- what you can't do --- it is particularly gratifying to witness those who defied being pigeon-holed. You don't have to be an average, normal, regular, common, everyday ANYTHING! This is a lesson that we, as should ALL people, learn as early in life as possible. After having been around for a while, seeing a few things, and witnessing the change, there is hope on the horizon, but the finish line still remains a distant dream. I see where Bernard Shaw (TV news anchor) passed away today. He was the inspiration for this one.

· · · · ·

Unless we make peace with our past, we will threaten the peace of our future.

· · · · ·

Random, though not likely original, thought: During the slave era, severe penalties were levied against anyone who dared teach slaves to read and write. But if slaves could be taught to read and write, how and why was the idea so widely taught, and accepted, that they were little more intellectually than animals --- incapable of thought and reason? That has to be one of the most sinister and destructive cases of self-deception in American history. The damaging effects haunt us to this day. The powers that be knew better then, still do now, and yet...

. . . . .

Those who would try to BAN history are actually attempting to HIDE history.

. . . . .

Think about something. In just about every one of the two hundred plus nations of this world, there is conflict of some kind because of "demographic differences" --- racial, religious, tribal, and a host of others --- all mere EXCUSES to justify mistreatment of the perceived "lesser" group in an amazingly CONSISTENT effort to justify "elevating" oneself above just another group of HUMAN BEINGS.

. . . . .

There are so many people in this country whose hatred of minorities remains so deep --- so visceral (relating to "feelings" rather than "intellect") --- that the likelihood of "turning" them, even toward common sense logic, is remote. God bless America, or God HELP America?

. . . . .

"The most dangerous person is the one who listens, thinks, and observes." - Bruce Lee

· · · · ·

As a child in the early 50's, it was easy to see that things were far from "equal" in this country. Being Black, there was an unabashed air of white supremacy all around me --- constantly. Countless methods were routinely employed to make Black people feel not only that that was the way it was, but also that that was the way it SHOULD be. As I grew older, the apparent urge (need?) to further that point grew also. Demonstrations, peaceful or violent, were met with the same intense hatred, unspeakable violence, imprisonment, and far too often, death. I often asked myself how I could best affect change in the things I saw. "How could I make life better for those who would come after me?" Getting it right meant walking a delicate tightrope, and for whatever difference I may have made, circumstances today remain disappointingly similar --- even depressing. Being told that things are "better than they once were" seems only a feeble attempt to inspire complacency. Equality must be total, or it is nothing. During all this time, the scourge of racism is, obviously, quite alive and well --- still deeply rooted in the bodies, minds, and yes, the very spirits of so many --- too many. Some remain so deeply marinated in it that I'm not likely to ever see its well-deserved demise. Four hundred years is a long time. Every now and again, I take a moment to rest, but no matter my fatigue, or my age, I dare not quit.

· · · · ·

The majority of the U.S. population, about 63%, is white. White people are not good (or bad) simply because they are white. Black people in America make up a bit less than 13% (about the same as Hispanics coincidentally). Black people are not good (or bad) simply because they are black. The majority of white people are GREAT PEOPLE. I've known quite a few, and that is my personal assessment. Like it or not, that's an accurate assessment. The majority of black people are GREAT PEOPLE. I've known quite a few, and that is my personal assessment. Like it or not, that's an accurate assessment. If you are white, when you think of blacks, do the first thoughts that come to mind involve crime, lewd music, welfare, saggy pants and such? If you are black, when you think of whites, do the first thoughts that come to mind involve racism, greed, privilege, power seeking and such? If the majority of whites are "good people," and the majority of blacks are "good people," why do we so often find ourselves judging the known majority by the actions of the known minority? If you are one of those who thinks this way, then YOU are what's wrong with America. If this sounds a bit "over-simplified," it is. The problem is not hard to identify, but why is it obviously so incredibly difficult to resolve? Human nature compels us to consider the NEGATIVE first. A 20-year flawless criminal record can be ruined by one misdemeanor. We naturally fight against, or refuse all together, to face who we really are, so there's a lot of "yeah buts" and "what abouts" that we employ in our, all-too-often successful, attempts to justify our respective stances on this touchy issue. Isn't that what makes it so "touchy" in the first place? Simplicity says, "Just consider the person's HEART," but it is a tough thing to look in the mirror and actually SEE what's there --- even tougher to act on the TRUTH that we see. Instead, we focus upon what "they might do to us", no matter the evidence of "goodness", so we do nothing --- or worse, we lash out, in a truly unbelievable variety of ways. It's not "them" we're afraid of; it's "us!"

· · · · ·

The heightened levels of hatred and racial tensions that we witness across America (the world) today are sending a clear message. If hate is growing, then steps to counter it must be (at least) commensurate. If not, then it's only logical that hatred will ultimately win. A shake of the head, a tsk-tsk, prayers, and condolences have never been enough. Stand up, or (continue to) be pushed aside --- run over. Love is a verb.

· · · · ·

Sometimes, it is good to be busy --- to have lots to do. These days afford me time to sit --- to look out of my favorite window at the grass and enjoy the little visitors who stop by to spend a moment. I am "blessed" with time to think about life and my own significance. In my quiet times, the thoughts push their way, uninvited and noisy, into my mind, even as it desperately seeks peace. I am helpless against it. I sometimes think about the history --- countless souls like myself --- Black and reared in this America --- the countless voices mercilessly silenced (incredible waste). "Where is God?" There are tears sometimes --- genuine, deep-down-in-the-chest pain that forces my head forward --- my face into my hands. "Swing Low, Sweet Chariot." They have not seen what I have seen; they cannot know what I know. For as long as I can remember, I have wanted to do something --- anything --- to at least make others more aware, but again, promotions, trinkets, and new cars get in the way --- sometimes. A bona fide old man now (the gray is there), reality says there is not much time. By all appearances, I will never see, much less know/feel, this freedom about which they sing --- boast. No pity needed --- a most disheartening thing --- sometimes. Still, I must stand. Others are coming. They will be watching.

· · · · ·

Some of the most cold-hearted massacres of innocents, like this last one, have involved shooters who, if they did not take their own lives, were captured alive (sometimes with weapons in hand) --- Boston, Charleston, El Paso, Buffalo, et al. Why has there been such a disproportionate percentage of black people who have been killed on site when they had no weapon and no intent to hurt anyone --- just trying to live. Ignoring the facts in no way diminishes their power or makes them go away.

. . . . .

Since it's cook-out season, it's good to remember that PEOPLE are also flavored by the times and spices in which they are marinated.

. . . . .

People tend to make of things what best suits their purposes. Some have convinced themselves that Black Lives Matter is some violent movement that's "out there" trying to overthrow the government, when, more than anything, its main purpose/message is a simple plea: "We're here; we count for something too." Yes, people will believe what they like. Sometimes, it's like talking to tree stumps though, and that is why I fish.

. . . . .

In college, I made my first trip abroad. Over a period of several months, I lived in a number of European countries. Interestingly, the Civil Rights Movement was still in full swing here. Back then, while it wasn't the coolest thang to be an African American, still ain't no cake-walk, lots of Europeans envied me --- ME! I was an AMERICAN after all, and it was still very cool to be an American, any kind. I still have many European friends. Most are not as enthusiastic about coming here as they once were though. Ironically, many still risk their lives to come to our shores, but these days, just as many risk their lives to stay here.

· · · · ·

It shouldn't be, but in many places, MIXED MARRIAGES are still considered unusual --- even peculiar. Mixed couples openly declare to the world that they have not bought into those incessant attempts to convince, brainwash, humans into believing the age-old cultural norm that one group of people is, in any way, "better" than another. Theirs is a very personal, deeply sincere "Declaration of Independence."

· · · · ·

It's hard to be sweet when you've been marinated in vinegar.

· · · · ·

JMHO --- All the money, and sympathy, in the world will never end racism, in this country or anywhere else. Offering such things as solutions is like pruning limbs from a huge tree whose roots are plentiful enough, deep enough, and strong enough to eventually stimulate regrowth. UNDERSTANDING is the key to unlocking those vital, essential nutrients --- forgiveness, kindness, mercy, selflessness --- difficult because the solution is ultimately a matter of the HEART. That, after all, is where the roots "lie."

• • • • •

It is both sad and amazing that, when it comes to racism, some people have been "marinated" in it for so long that it is no longer the fact that they WON'T see both sides of the issue, but that they CAN'T. That's why the challenge is so huge.

• • • • •

Why is it that you rarely (if ever) see Black daredevils? Simple. We work too hard just trying to stay alive, every day, to risk said lives so unnecessarily. (JMHO)

• • • • •

When the body is seriously wounded, infection becomes a very real concern. If ignored, it spreads through the bloodstream to other parts of the body, causing possible amputations and even death. Slavery was a severe wound in this nation's history. Racism is the virulent infection. It has never been effectively --- thoroughly --- treated, so like all infections, it did not --- could not --- simply "go away." The shame lies in having the proper disinfectants/dressings for all these years and refusing to apply them.

· · · · ·

Imagine what pioneers like Jackie Robinson, Mae Jemison, Sydney Portier, and countless other "firsts" must have felt as they, after the usual trials and persecutions, witnessed the fruits of their labors. Thanks to their efforts, distant dreams became reality. Others decided, "Hey, I can do that too," and the rest, as they say, is history --- the struggle, apparently well worth it. In every sphere of influence: politics, sports, entertainment, business, religion, and all the rest, it's true. To live long enough (it has been a slog) to see representation in all fields of endeavor must be wonderfully gratifying for those who first dared. It is sad, however, that beautiful concepts like justice and freedom can also generate very genuine --- often life-threatening --- FEARS.

· · · · ·

Human beings are, by nature, SOCIAL creatures. Like bees and deer, they function best and are happiest when they are together in groups, depending (not always directly) upon each other. RELATIONSHIPS --- a key ingredient in the recipe of life --- are essential to survival. Their creation, maintenance, and development require FAITH and TRUST. Aggression and deceit among races and cultures have eroded faith and trust, severely damaging the very relationships that add color to the world. So, humanity often finds itself stumbling about in dull, multiple shades of gray. When conspiracy theories abound, some groups may feel justified in denying the right of others to even exist. Fear, suspicion, and mistrust, are stirred into the recipe, and any hope of finding true peace, love, and happiness in the world is lost, and people are left longing for the comfort and safety of the hive/herd.

· · · · ·

A former student (just one more favorite) just shared an interesting message. It might clear away the fog, and help people see things a bit more clearly. Several people have asked me about Critical Race Theory (CRT) --- what it is, what I think, etc. There was a recent quote from Congressman Tom Cotton praising Jackie Robinson for having broken the color barrier in major league baseball some 75 years ago. "We honor him and his lasting legacy." In response to what appears to be a very complimentary statement came the question: "Should students learn why he wasn't allowed to play?" Nothing more really needs to be said.

• • • • •

Imagine being a black citizen (if you're not already) living in Anywhere, USA. Imagine going to school, elementary to university, shopping, any kind, anywhere, a concert, a movie, a restaurant, a club, a hotel, an airport, your backyard, your living room, or your bedroom (you get the idea). You MUST develop a third eye, and it MUST (always) see 20/20. Now, imagine living 70 years.

• • • • •

RACISM is an octopus with a thousand tentacles. Be patient. With so many suckers, this is going to take a while.

• • • • •

If you know people who bristle at the sight or mention of anything "Black Lives Matter", and chances are you do, know this: They may make the usual excuses --- Antifa affiliations, violence, looting & burning --- but their issues likely run much deeper and are far more sinister than that. Don't just look --- SEE.

• • • • •

Ever notice how racism and greed almost always appear to be joined at the hip?

· · · · ·

If you are an American of color, you WILL have to fight racism --- possibly every day of your life. If you are a white American, you WILL have to fight racism --- possibly every day of your life. On one hand, you have a choice; on the other, none.

· · · · ·

Historically (hysterically), when and how did mankind decide DIVERSITY is a "bad" thing?

· · · · ·

I'll bet you have walked into a business establishment where someone there, customers and/or employees, immediately began to "size you up." Without a word, and often unaware, they "analyze" you --- judging you by your dress, your gender, your age, or of course, your race so they can decide whether or not you're worth their time or consideration. Don't be "that person."

· · · · ·

During the era of Jim Crow and segregation, overt racism was the norm --- expected --- reliable as sunrise. I knew the meaning of poverty back then, so I also knew hunger and shoeless feet. I remember the desire for "normal" things ---

toys at Christmas, to travel outside the state. Like everyone, I too wanted to be somebody. I didn't know it then, but it was hardship that would help me gain a true sense of IDENTITY. The old people around me, none of them college educated, were wise. They were survivors. They provided the smooth stones for me to hurl back at a world that hurled insults in its attempt to convince me who I wasn't --- that dreams of the "good life" would, for me, forever remain just that --- dreams. The world nearly succeeded. Looking back, I relish those struggles, and not just my own, but those of my family, neighbors, and friends. Difficult times taught me a most precious lesson. I felt compelled to teach it to everyone I could. Others could be overcomers too, even in a world that would forever try to crush them.

· · · · ·

If you are a minority and consider yourself successful in this America (a survivor), then you have likely spent a good portion of your life teaching --- a "perpetual instructor" in a huge classroom of either eager/curious students, for whom you are deeply grateful, or other, close-minded ones who refuse to see (let alone accept) the great potential benefits of learning about each other.

· · · · ·

Human beings can find all sorts of things to do in life, but arguably, the worst (and the biggest waste of time) is HATING.

· · · · ·

How many of us THINK, "better together," but betray its truth every day?

· · · · ·

Decades ago, when I was just a schoolboy, things were, not surprisingly, very different. In the midst of an era when segregation was the norm, it never occurred to me that I had been born frighteningly close --- less than one century actually --- to the much tougher era of SLAVERY. To this day, I remember the lyrics of the "Old Negro Spirituals" --- some of which, with the full knowledge and encouragement of teachers and administration, we proudly sang in those classrooms amid the distinctive aromas of pencil shavings, the large jars of peppermint paste, construction paper, and those huge crayons. Some of you will identify. I guess they thought it was important. In some of those songs, slaves sang about welcoming death and anticipating the joys of the afterlife --- one that simply had to be much better than their Earthly existence. "Swing Low, Sweet Chariot" comes to mind.

· · · · ·

Sadly, leadership today, of this and other countries as well, tends to disregard the suffering of the people as much, if not more, than ever. Perhaps it is wrong of me to think in such a way, but I find solace in the thought that, one fine day, leaders, too, will come face-to-face with their Maker, some having callously padded their own pockets during their earthly stay. I want so much to be angry with them for their wanton disregard of so much hurt --- so much suffering --- but as my anger rises within me, it is somehow overcome --- replaced --- with other, more powerful emotions --- PITY, FORGIVENESS. It is only then that I know I will --- MUST --- endure. And I am comforted.

· · · · ·

Anyone can agree that racism is a huge problem in this country --- a simple and well-known fact. When facing a problem, the absolute worst thing to do is to deny its existence or promote ignorance about that existence. How else can people expect to discover solutions? You CANNOT fix a problem that you don't know exists."

· · · · ·

Having to endure a lifetime of slights, insults, and various abuses can be truly exhausting. For some of us, it is all we've ever known. As I arrive at what might be considered a ripe old age, I sometimes find myself quite ready to leave this world, and finally be rid of so many pointless, but necessary, concerns. Looking back, I hope and pray I might have made some small difference in things --- some positive contribution to an oblivious world. So many today stubbornly hold on to a belief system that casually tosses nails and broken glass onto the path that I am obliged to walk. I realized long ago how much it costs to care. How am I to feel as I see a black child holding up a sign recently? "My Life Matters," it read. I am reminded of a sign I saw held aloft by an elderly black man during the struggle for civil rights more than 60 years ago: "I Am A Man," it read. No matter the claims of honor, of liberty --- of glory --- it is truly sad that ANY citizen of ANY society ANYWHERE should ever feel the need to publicly profess such a desperate message. "Oh, say can you see?"

· · · · ·

My father was, perhaps by necessity, a history buff. He would have loved to live long enough to see this country elect its first black president. His last words to me: --- "Boy, ya gotta HELP somebody in this world." All my life, I've tried to do just that. I would love to live long enough to see the end of racism in this country. It is terribly disheartening to realize that my children will most likely not live long enough to witness that one either.

· · · · ·

Hemlock, cyanide, arsenic, ricin, novichok --- you may be more familiar with some of these than others, but when it comes to a poison's downright deadliness, not one of them can top HATRED.

· · · · ·

"My hand is not the color of yours, but if I pierce it, I shall feel pain. If you pierce your hand, you also feel pain. The blood that will flow from mine will be the same color as yours. The same God made us both." --- Standing Bear, Ponca Chief (1879) Too often, and to our great detriment, we ignore such wisdom --- simple, powerful truths.

· · · · ·

AMERICA --- THE BLACK AND WHITE OF IT: You've heard it said --- "In our house, our parents didn't raise us to be racist. They taught us to treat everybody the same, no matter their skin color." Even where that may be true, nobody spends his lifetime under one roof. At school, at work, and at social gatherings (especially), everybody "hears things" about those "others." The stares and the "involuntary social distancing", even at young ages, are very apparent giveaways, and that's true of the vast majority of us. It is impossible to be insulated from the many racial innuendos --- derogatory things people say about those "not like us." Segregation, because of its very definition, propagates ignorance, and can only serve to strengthen ill-informed beliefs. No direct association provides no evidence to disprove even the wildest claims. The detrimental effects of those forced isolations still plague us today. The media, social and otherwise, has not helped. If, for example, the public sees a preponderance of crime in the country being committed by one race, then the public will eventually be convinced that criminals form a major part of their population. Of course, the same may be said for any number of things, intelligence being a major one. Though many were taught to fear integration, exposure and experience (as always) bring enlightenment and wisdom. It has been a painfully SLOW process, and though there are some who stubbornly cling to old, misguided beliefs, white people in greater numbers are beginning to see that black people are simply darker-skinned versions of themselves --- certainly not worthy of the injustices to which, for centuries, they have been subjected. Likewise, black people are finally beginning to see white people as simply lighter-skinned versions of themselves --- that, more and more of them are willing to be honest with themselves about the realities of race in this country. While this is true, those sinister elements, born of racist ideologies, stubbornly persist, and sadly, sometimes reveal themselves in tragic ways. You have already seen more than enough evidence. It doesn't really matter where you live in America. You WILL eventually be exposed to racism at some level, and sometimes to the extreme. The challenge lies in what you decide to do about it. More and more people are realizing just how hazardous it can be to turn a blind eye --- pretend it doesn't exist, that it will eventually "go away." That attitude has, repeatedly, invited this demon to rear its ugly head and announce that it is not only here, but here to stay if we are not willing to stand strong against it. The lines have been clearly drawn in the sand. Search yourself. Like it or not, there is no gray area.

· · · · ·

I'm certainly no advocate of segregation, but back in the day, integration brought with it more than its share of challenges. In my first year of college, it was not only encouraging but very inspiring just to see another student who looked like me. On such a huge campus, our numbers were so small that personal encounters were rather uncommon, if not rare. Seeing each other, therefore, was genuine cause for excitement, celebration? --- no words were necessary; the message was consistent --- clear. A simple smile and a wave said so much --- "Hang in there; You're gonna make it. You're not alone." It was still difficult, but the encouragement was precious--- appreciated. We instinctively knew we were fighting our own individual, often unseen, battles. During my sophomore year, the only other black athlete in the dorm, Charlie, and I decided to jump into his car and drive down to North Carolina A&T for their homecoming festivities. We relished the chance to be close to so many who looked like us. Interestingly, they had no idea how much they were appreciated that day. Charlie and I just looked at each other and smiled. We got back in his car for the return trip, each to face very real, very fierce competition (on the basketball court, on the track, and wherever else we might find ourselves) when we got back.

· · · · ·

Being racist doesn't really mean what some think. Racists sadly convince themselves that God makes mistakes.

· · · · ·

Have you ever watched hurdle events in track and field? Have you ever asked yourself why in the world anybody would ever want to DO that? I'm biased, but I think it's the most beautiful event in all of track and field. It takes so many different skills to get really good at it: strength, quickness, speed, flexibility, timing, agility, courage, determination, coachability, intelligence, humility and in a way, maybe a little insanity too. It is a difficult event to run well, and arguably, an even more difficult one to coach. Because it requires every body part to move in a perfectly coordinated fashion, the opportunities for error are plentiful. But mistakes can be totally oblivious to the hurdlers themselves. They often have no awareness at all of any of them.

· · · · ·

Good coaches are essential. In fact, they must have many of the same qualities as their charges. In many ways, ridding a nation of racism is a lot like that. You could easily come up with at least a half dozen similarities between those two scourges of humanity --- RACISM and CANCER. One of them, however, often carries with it an additional, sinister quality --- CONTAGIOUS.

· · · · ·

Growing up Black in this world, since the '50s, has been, in many ways, an eye-opener. I've learned, quite well, the meaning of hatred, but from it, I've also learned many profound life lessons. If death appears on the horizon to those who hate, it often, but not always, morphs into genuine sorrow and regret --- a strange "awakening" as they contemplate that long "slumber." Apologies are rare, and strangely unnecessary, as visions of eternity can reveal truth better than the wisest among us. The eyes must surely be the windows to the soul.

· · · · ·

If you carefully watch someone's behavior long enough --- what they say and do --- you can usually tell where their perceptions of God and spirituality lie.

· · · · ·

When associated with certain words, simple prepositions can be powerful. There's a huge difference between "freedom TO" and "freedom FROM."

· · · · ·

It's been said that one of Satan's most effective tactics is to deny his own existence. Too many still believe similar claims about racism.

· · · · ·

Being Black in America is sometimes a lot like trying to cross a 12-lane highway at rush hour. It was easier (but more dangerous) to cross when I was younger, nimble, and more agile. Now that I'm older, I've grown more patient. I now know which I prefer.

· · · · ·

Is it that you don't see, or that you do see, but just don't care?

THE WORLD

Flawed, Fraud, Oh Gawd

It is heartrending to see the suffering --- the cruelty of war --- that's being endured in this world. How do you think they will ever rebuild their countries? Even quaint, old villages have been leveled. I pray for a mild winter.

· · · · ·

When you look at the personal lives of those who are killed in mass shootings, it seems unfair that perpetrators get to spend the rest of THEIR lives locked away on the taxpayers' dime, while victims and their loved ones are left to find ways to cope with the unimaginable. It is particularly heartrending when the victims are children. This is not a message backing capital punishment, but rather a plea for an effective way to keep such lethal weapons out of the hands of those who obviously don't share our value for human life. Some believe it is a matter of mental illness. In some cases it is, but in any case, we are left with two choices --- find some way to fix it or simply ignore it in the hope that it will eventually "go away." With these incidents becoming an almost everyday occurrence, we can only hope one of those choices is becoming increasingly more unthinkable.

· · · · ·

This election is like a fishing expedition. The goal, of course, is to catch "the big one" (POWER). It's interesting how the primary issues of the day --- the economy, abortion, etc. are simply "bait" --- all trophies to be awarded back at the dock.

· · · · ·

When you consider the incredible strides that humanity has made in all areas of "technological advancement" --- medicine, construction, sciences, and many others --- just over the past century, it is truly mind-boggling. And although there have been definite signs of improvement in this one key area, it is almost depressing that we have come no further than we have in all those areas that deal with the simple matter of HOW WE TREAT EACH OTHER.

· · · · ·

It doesn't take a genius to realize the difference between "truths" and "lies." Perhaps more than ever, the world is learning grievous lessons through the incredible power of both.

. . . . .

Have you ever in your life known a time when the difference between FACT & FICTION was so clouded --- when the OBVIOUS goes so totally unseen --- so unacknowledged? The nation may well be in far deeper trouble than we realize.

. . . . .

When we were little, my younger brother and I were typical siblings. We'd squabble and fight almost every day. One day, a neighbor's kid, a known bully, started pushing my brother around. He was older and bigger than I was, but I pulled him off of my brother and beat him up. He ran home. (His mother witnessed the whole thing through a window. She thanked me.) There is a lot wrong with this country. In the eyes of many, we are the most powerful nation in the world, in history --- true --- but we are also violent, greedy, and discriminatory. We tout our first amendment rights, but criticizing the country's very real shortcomings can inspire retaliation like little else, moving some to retribution that often includes hatred and violence. It's interesting how we draw social lines. Gerrymandering is really a form of bullying and isn't just about maps.

. . . . .

"Fair is foul and foul is fair." Shakespeare was right. This "inversion of values" has become pandemic --- more than ever, the rule rather than the exception. Truth is scorned, and facts have become "alternative." Deceit is now praiseworthy, leaving the masses drowning in ignorance, confusion --- derangement. At the slightest touch, violence erupts --- everyone swinging wildly at each other, and often for no legitimate reason. Mercy and kindness have been relegated to the backseat --- while former virtues like honesty and integrity appear to have gone the way of the dodo. Is this some new thing, or is this who we've been all along?

· · · · ·

No one wants to sound like a "prophet of doom", the thoughts are likely swirling around in your head too, but when I consider all the turmoil in the world these days: Ukraine, Israel, Gaza (the ravages of war --- its global impact), natural disasters (earthquakes, floods), atrocities galore (horrific shootings --- mass, school, suicide), global warming (fires, melting polar regions), and the perpetual, raging geo-political climate, one word keeps coming to mind --- PRECIPICE. Looking over the edge, what do YOU see? Gives new meaning to optimism and pessimism, doesn't it?

· · · · ·

Years ago, I was privileged to spend some time in Russia. During those weeks, educator that I was, I noticed some interesting things --- the beauty of the snowfall (soot-covered by the very next day); the total absence of wild animal tracks (even in the forests); the curious absence of wind (even at the beach). My host family, wonderfully kind people, appeared content with their "existence", not "living" as we know it, --- satisfied to snatch whatever joy they could from "simple pleasures." When you don't know --- when you're not told --- ignorance reigns and becomes dangerous because it makes it easier to CONTROL MINDS, and FEAR becomes a far more potent tool. That truth applies in more places than Russia.

· · · · ·

Many are unaware that Henry Aaron received nearly a million hate letters --- threats on his life, as well as those of his family members --- if he dared to break the home run record of the great Babe Ruth. Aaron never wavered. He took extra precautions, but he broke the record anyway. It's both shocking and disappointing these days that so many public servants, local to federal, are also being threatened with violence for doing their jobs honorably. (A U.S. senator recently received death threats for his 5-month-old son.) In such a volatile climate, some officials are choosing to retire from public service. I am no hero --- certainly no Henry

Aaron --- but personally, I never liked bullies. If it came down to "them or me," well...

. . . . .

In life, it is good to keep watch over the role that struggle, pain, and suffering play, and to keep it in proper perspective. After championship competitions, athletes often refer to what it took to achieve that coveted victory. Successful business people refer to humble beginnings --- all that it took to make it to the top. Each of us has his own row to hoe --- some (most) involve more sweat equity, and sometimes more tears than others. Sooner or later --- inevitably --- life WILL throw the gauntlet at your feet, sometimes unexpectedly, sometimes even violently, and you are obliged to respond. Always --- ALWAYS --- you will have CHOICES. You may run away in fear, or you may pick it up, stronger for having done so. It is best to remember that life, all by itself, is tough enough, but most often, you're not.

. . . . .

Watch how those around you respond to adversity. Our country faces huge challenges right now. Some complain, some point fingers, and still others stand and fight that proverbial good fight. On which team do you choose to play?

. . . . .

As we witness the truly frightening circumstances going on around the world, the variety and severity of the struggle and suffering might convince you that the entire earth is turning against its human inhabitants. And all the while, the rich and powerful remain insatiable, obsessed with enriching themselves in whatever way they can. Incredibly selfish, greedy, prideful, cruel, and indifferent, they know those who act in such a manner deserve to be condemned, and yet... They have gone so far in their destructive ways that it seems the earth itself has turned against us --- understandable. We have become like so many termites squabbling over the last splinter of wood. Maybe the solution was too simple; all we had to do was love one another. Still, we dare not give up on that one because the "or else" now seems more ominous than ever.

·　·　·　·　·

International Holocaust Remembrance Day and we wonder how hatred can still remain such a huge factor in so many of our dealings with each other.

·　·　·　·　·

People find all kinds of ways to cope with the insanity in this world. I can't speak for you, but I fret and mess up a lot, so, especially THESE days, I talk to God a lot.

$\cdot\ \cdot\ \cdot\ \cdot\ \cdot$

Consider: Hundreds of thousands of Russia's top intellectuals have fled the country --- never to return. In time, the crushing effects of unprecedented sanctions will start to weigh upon everyone, and likely worsen for decades to come. Tens of thousands of Russian fighters will not be coming home. Their women/mothers have witnessed this before. Russia and "pariah" are at once synonymous --- despised by the world. The horrible things you see, and the terrible stories you hear --- all the suffering and death --- caused by one man --- a hefty price to pay to satisfy one ego that will never be satisfied.

$\cdot\ \cdot\ \cdot\ \cdot\ \cdot$

It seems that no matter how hard we try, harmful human behavior will never be completely eradicated. The drug culture, the sexual revolution, the gun culture, and all the rest, are proof that, with freedoms, more and more freedoms are demanded --- ever more liberties to do whatever, even when the demands might cause harm to innocent others. The human body will forever fight this malignant tumor, and once the symptoms become apparent, it can be a huge struggle to regain control. That tumor can never be totally excised. It can only be "treated" --- controlled, limited. Ignored, it quickly gets out of control --- the results of which can be devastating. That's why nations institute policies, regulations, and all sorts of laws. If not, the tumor will eventually ensure that chaos reigns. This has been true everywhere throughout history. In the human psyche, the concept of liberty can be so strong that efforts to place/enforce restrictions upon it are often met with violence. Left unchecked, entire cultures have literally freed themselves to death. Where, how, are people to draw the lines? There are a thousand shades of gray, and each society must choose. Most will forever find it difficult, if not entirely impossible, to choose the right one. Sunday morning thoughts --- just my opinions.

· · · · ·

Corruption, violence, unprecedented cruelty: Have you given much thought to just how little there is that shocks/surprises you these days?

· · · · ·

FLAWED or FRAUD --- huge difference.

· · · · ·

It was the great SHOWMAN, P. T. Barnum who (in the mid-19th century) said, "There's a sucker born every minute." I'll just leave that right there.

You've probably noticed how much EVIL there is in the world these days. How could you not? There's a long list of modifiers to describe some of the bad things people do --- horrific, grisly, dreadful, you could add more. You've probably gotten yourself all worked up over the fact that evildoers often seem to "get away with it" too, but when you think about it, that doesn't seem to be true at all. Mean people ALWAYS "get theirs," and there is genuine comfort in that thought. Normal human beings find it difficult to be PATIENT when JUSTICE is on the line.

. . . . .

The cold-blooded murder of worshippers, no matter the faith, demonstrates a new level of depravity. It should make us wonder who we are becoming, or perhaps who we already are. It's ridiculous to think God needs our help to run the world. JMHO

. . . . .

It would seem that, with the many posts during this last election cycle, as soon as someone establishes an "us vs. them" paradigm in their statements, there is no need to read anything further. Terms like republican, democrat, liberal, conservative, progressive, Tea Partier, etc. all seem to be clear indicators that the speaker (writer) has already dug his/her heels in the sand, or into the other person's throat, be they friend, family, or total stranger, and the chance of any civil discourse is drastically reduced or eliminated altogether --- little hope of any peaceful resolution at all. I don't think anyone was prepared for just how exhausting this could be. With all the controversy that continues to swirl, it doesn't appear likely to end any time soon either. These times may be described in a multitude of ways, but "DULL" is not likely to be one of them.

· · · · ·

In life, it's ironic that mankind can be both the ultimate blessing and the ultimate curse --- CHOICES.

· · · · ·

With the aid of this new James Webb telescope, scientists believe they have discovered a planet, about the size of Jupiter, in a distant galaxy. Interestingly, they think that planet may very possibly have WATER VAPOR in its atmosphere. That thought kicks your brain in gear, doesn't it? The only problem is that planet lies a mere one thousand lightyears away. I won't bore you with all the calculations, but, logically, a lightyear is the DISTANCE light travels in a YEAR (at a speed of approximately 186,000 miles per SECOND --- times 60 to get miles per MINUTE, then times another to get miles per HOUR). Then, of course, you'll need to multiply that number by another thousand. Yes, I have Excedrin in hand. So there's all this information way out there that you can't possibly ever know --- zillions of bits of information to ponder. It's all quite fascinating, but I can't help wondering how much difference it might make in adding SIGNIFICANCE to the fact that you ever existed? I love learning as much as the next person, but my goodness!

· · · · ·

At least locally, it's a good day to sit and look out of your favorite window.

· · · · ·

While you are not responsible for the actions of your ancestors, you ARE responsible for understanding how their actions (continue to) affect today's belief systems.

· · · · ·

It doesn't apply in ALL cases, of course, but for a good many of the problems this nation faces, the average citizen can offer practical, logical solutions. How is it that so many politicians can get it so wrong so often, sometimes even convincing the citizenry (as well as each other) not to even trust common sense?

. . . . .

Power --- Privilege --- PRINCIPLE.

. . . . .

It's not comfortable --- might even be dangerous --- but this country is beginning to slowly admit and confront its habitual hypocrisy. It will be interesting to see where this leads.

. . . . .

This area, Tidewater, includes more than seven cities. It is a military mecca; every branch of our armed forces is well represented: Army, Navy, Air Force, Marines, Coast Guard --- even NASA! Though it can get a bit noisy at times, one of the most wonderful benefits is that we get to see lots of returns from deployments. What is it about seeing little ones running across the huge, shiny concrete floors of giant hangars, or out onto tarmacs next to sophisticated aircraft, or onto huge piers next to truly gigantic ships --- and falling into the arms of daddies and mommies? It just turns everybody red, white, and blue. Then, there are spouses, boyfriends, and girlfriends. This can be a highly emotional place.

. . . . .

Nobody mentions it much, enough, but this country lost more than one million of its citizens (and counting) due to COVID. While that is certainly painful enough, this disease has also changed just about everything else. Education, employment, recreation --- every facet of what was once considered "normal," is all very different now. It is strange how two plus years of hibernation seem to have accelerated time itself.

· · · · ·

In horror movies, why are purity and innocence the usual victims? Why does pure evil consistently seek to martyr them? It's true in vampire lore; it was true during the crucifixion, and it's true today.

· · · · ·

What happens in a country where there are more guns than there are people? Exactly what we are witnessing today. Have we become so red, white, and **GREEN** that we are still willing to turn a blind eye to this catastrophic loss of life? If you are not angry, then you must already dwell among the dead.

· · · · ·

As a nation, we are at a point where some things now require serious consideration. We grew up singing "America the Beautiful," reciting the Pledge of Allegiance, and singing the National Anthem. We were wonderfully patriotic in appearance, as much of that was pretense. More than a few unpleasant historical facts, in time, have come to light, and though painful, they are clear. With the revelations, the question then becomes, what do we do with them? Some will continue attempts to hide them, and others will continue to deny them altogether, but some will face them. They are the ones who realize that is ultimately the only way to become that "light on a hill that cannot be hidden" --- the nation that, since our founding, we have proudly professed to be: "ONE NATION UNDER GOD WITH LIBERTY AND JUSTICE FOR ALL." Truth or consequences --- the pleas have been many; let each decide.

· · · · ·

By definition, FEAR and FAITH cannot operate on the same plane. It is interesting how so many self-proclaimed believers can be so easily terrorized by our overabundance of doomsday prophets.

· · · · ·

I still remember the public outrage at the sight of Elvis' gyrating hips on the Ed Sullivan Show. That was back in 1956, during an era where CHEWING GUM was the most serious, common offense by students in public schools.

Public outrage surely has changed. We've come a long way, haven't we? (Being sarcastic here)

· · · · ·

We continue to get heartbreaking reports of natural disasters in various parts of the world. Today, I am saddened by yet another tragic weather disaster in Puerto Rico. Citizens there had not yet fully recovered from damages by hurricane Maria. I am also reminded of a family whose sons, years ago, I was privileged to teach. The eldest, from day one, was a particular favorite. His time in my Spanish class was understandably more a study of grammar than speaking --- much like American students take English classes. He was incredibly quick-witted and fun-loving. I enjoyed the time we spent in class immensely. I remember when his loving parents passed away. He also lost a brother (drunk driver), but despite what could have been major life setbacks, he went on to champion the rights of the Latino community in the North Carolina area where he lives --- a priority for him to this day. He is a school administrator, apparently a very good one, and I couldn't be more proud of him, his wife, and their two wonderful kids. I don't know all the black belt degrees in karate, but he is "up there" --- very accomplished. He and his wife visited some years back to pay his respects to the grave of his beloved "Sensei", and I didn't miss the opportunity to meet with them to chat for a while. It should come as no surprise that his lifelong hero is Chuck Norris.

· · · · ·

In boxing, there is a term, "punch drunk" --- brain injury from repeated blows to the head. It occurs in football too, but the term is considerably more "sophisticated" --- chronic traumatic encephalopathy (CTE). You may now add Uvalde to Columbine, Sandy Hook, Blacksburg, Parkland, and too many others. Mass shootings are always horrific, but SCHOOL shootings, especially so. The thought of children lying there --- gunned down --- is traumatic, but the effects cause even more severe brain injury --- those families, the first responders, the faculty/staff, and those of us whose hearts still function. These incidents tear at the very soul. How do we rid ourselves of this curse; how do we recover? Headgear for the heart? Body armor for the spirit?

· · · · ·

Fred Astaire, Ginger Rogers, and Bill "Bojangles" Robinson were all gifted dancers, but they had nothing on modern-day politicians.

· · · · ·

It's election time again, and everybody is scrutinizing candidates --- doing their best to convince themselves that their assessments are accurate. I am no exception. I consider myself a fair judge of character but find myself questioning my judgments --- what I actually see and hear --- because it appears to run contrary to that of so many others. I'm fishing more than ever these days.

· · · · ·

Once upon a time, political parties debated POLICY & PROCEDURE. Debate topics have now shifted to matters of CHARACTER & PERSONALITY, and again, the PEOPLE suffer.

· · · · ·

When we elect leaders lacking in that paramount quality of good leadership, CHARACTER, we earn the sorrowful rewards for our own negligence.

· · · · ·

Nobody talks about it much, certainly not publicly, but it is fascinating how all the turmoil going on in the country these days has revealed what's REALLY in the hearts of some of those we thought we knew.

· · · · ·

IMHO: I have examined this gun controversy issue from every angle I know. I've heard any number of suggested resolutions, from the reasonable to the ridiculous. I have seen polls reflecting what the majority of America (and the world) thinks. I HAVE SEEN MANY INNOCENT PEOPLE DIE - SO MANY OF THEM, PRECIOUS CHILDREN. I have studied measures other countries have taken, some, admittedly extreme. In my opinion, assault weapons do not need to be in the hands of the general public. Removing them won't eliminate the problem, but the number of such shootings would definitely go down. One thing is certain; the problem isn't going to just go away. Well-known saying: "To do the same thing, in this case, nothing, and expect different outcomes is the definition of insanity."

· · · · ·

Forensic personnel had to collect DNA from the parents to help identify some of the victims at Uvalde --- mostly little ones. We can assume the same was true after Sandy Hook (and others). People really need to keep that thought at the forefront of their minds, and not push it into the far reaches of them.

· · · · ·

When did we decide CHARACTER means so little when it comes to LEADERSHIP?

· · · · ·

If your neighbor's home caught fire, you'd have several options: call 9-1-1, make sure no one was inside, if there were, help them out if possible, or you could sit and watch it burn. Our children are being slaughtered and some are choosing to roast hotdogs and toast marshmallows, debating their appropriate level of doneness.

· · · · ·

There is certainly a lot of wrong going on in the world today --- civil rights, gun rights, voting rights, economy, education, crime, politics, corruption, and a whole slew of others. Focus on them too much, however, and they can totally ruin your eyesight.

· · · · ·

LEADERSHIP: Intimidation or Inspiration?

· · · · ·

In 1982, futurist and inventor R. Buckminster Fuller estimated "that up until 1900, human knowledge doubled every century, but by 1945, it was doubling every 25 years. By 1982, it was doubling every 12-13 months."

· · · · ·

We have gone from the Wright Brothers to stealth bombers, to space tourism in about 120 years. If knowledge has increased that much that fast, how do we explain the condition in which we find ourselves today? Was Darth Vader right? Have we gone over to the Dark Side?

· · · · ·

Debate is pointless when opponents know they are wrong, but just don't care.

· · · · ·

When I was stationed at Fort Benning, GA back in 1972, a prisoner named Lt. Richard Calley had been tried and sentenced for war crimes and was housed there. He had been convicted of leading a massacre in a small Vietnamese village called My Lai. Tragically, many civilian women and children were among the dead. Our soldiers put their lives on the line every day in training and in war, just as our police officers do. As with Lt. Calley, however, the misdeeds of ONE individual can give a black eye to the VAST MAJORITY who daily go beyond the call of duty to serve with courage and honor. The incredible stress of that (any) war can cause good soldiers to "go bad." Police officers routinely fight a never-ending war too --- an ENDLESS, progressively more "dirty" war --- but there are "rules of war" by which they, like soldiers, are also sworn to abide. Occasionally, the stress gets to a few, and it can manifest itself in a number of ways. (Remember, an American war veteran dies by his/her own hand every hour of every day.) War is always a tough job. Soldiers and police officers are trained to identify "the enemy," and to respond APPROPRIATELY. If Lt. Calley had suspicions about those in My Lai, then there should have been POW's --- not orders for extra body bags. Let us RESPECT our officers, as we do our soldiers, but let us be diligent and fair about bringing justice to those few who might, for whatever reason, overstep (abuse) their authority. Police officers and soldiers are, as are we all, human beings --- flawed and subject to err --- and because of that one fact, WE should, as tough as it is sometimes, be prepared to forgive, if only for our own sanity, as the families of the slain in Charleston did with Dylan Roof. "RIGHT" don't always mean "easy."

· · · · ·

One of my brother Jack's favorite sayings: "Peace is not in the DNA of mankind." I was never able to disprove that one.

· · · · ·

It may be the ultimate demonstration of capitalism that (especially with the popularity of social media) businesses have begun to mass produce TOXICITY and market it to the world.

· · · · ·

It seems more people than ever believe it's all right to act all wrong.

· · · · ·

Al Qaeda, ISIS, Boko Haram, Abu Sayyaf: What images come to mind when you hear the word --- "terrorist?" Russian soldiers invaded Ukraine recently. Perhaps you didn't think to include them, but they fit the description perfectly. The main goal of terrorists is, naturally, "to terrify" --- to instill fear in the hearts and minds of others, mostly innocents. Cruelty, violence, and ruthlessness are common calling cards. When we think of terrorists, we usually think of "foreigners," yet, terrorism has, for centuries, been very much a domestic issue. What images come to mind when someone mentions "domestic" terrorism? We have the granddaddy of them all, the KKK, and relatively new kids on the block --- the Proud Boys, the Oath Keepers, et al. They have only recently been referred to as terrorists, but they fit the description perfectly too. (Sadly, some law enforcement officers have been counted among their ranks.) Their goal is also to instill fear --- terror --- in the hearts (and minds) of others (mostly innocents). Cruelty, violence, and ruthlessness are their calling cards as well. LIFE is a GIFT from GOD. We have become incredibly careless --- reckless --- in our dealings with it. In fact, we have been all too willing (any ol' time) to take that priceless gift away (as if God needs OUR help to make this world a better place). It is such a waste --- a travesty. We "discard" lives as if they were worthless bits of garbage. There is great wisdom in learning to love one another. Especially recently, we have been miserable failures at it. Instead, too many are drawn into cults of hatred. We are not in a good place. It will be interesting to see how all this plays out. I hope and pray I am here to witness the other side of all this.

• • • • •

Have you stopped to ask yourself why such an amazing outpouring of concern, prayer --- LOVE --- for a professional athlete whose name most had never even heard? THAT'S the "human being" in us --- who we should all be at all times. Now, think about the petty squabbles, so common within our leadership, that cause so much suffering and anguish. If we apparently know who we're SUPPOSED to be, then who, what, where, when, why?

• • • • •

It appears the war on justice, fairness, and all that's "good" has heated up. This is no time to "relax on the sidelines."

Because those who think like the men who killed that young black man are prone to be vocal and, obviously, violent, it takes courage to stand against them. If we haven't the courage to stand up against such obvious wrongs, then we shouldn't even have the right to call ourselves Americans.

· · · · ·

The thing that makes common sense issues so common is that they are so widely known and accepted as true. When the validity --- soundness, legitimacy --- of such issues is denied or ignored, it births the need for a new term --- not "willful," but "WONTFUL!"

· · · · ·

Everywhere across the land --- this, and any number of others, the conversations have begun yet again --- some quite heated, and justifiably so. From the highest levels of government to the living rooms, workplaces, and every imaginable media platform, people are talking. Since our birth as a nation a little more than two centuries ago, we have become famous for our monuments, our great variety of fun spots --- our many natural wonders. Then, there is our greatest claim to fame --- our sheer POWER --- even to destroy every living thing on earth, dozens of times over. Perhaps as an unintended result, rampant violence has now become our trademark, not exactly anyone's favorite "tourist attraction". Still, the debates rage on. The thoughts and prayers continue to be dispatched like clockwork, only to cool a bit --- 'til the next time. Is God really listening? As horrific as the events are, why must there always be a "next one?" How can we not be convinced that this may NOT have been God's plan? Whatever can (will) we do? So many debates --- so many arguments --- and so few solutions or genuine efforts to implement any. Deep inside, we know what will work, but leadership, for its own reasons, will not find the courage to stand against thrown rocks, even as the blood runs freely in our streets, our schools --- our homes. The greatest civilizations collapsed from the inside --- internal rot --- violence, corruption, greed, deception, and other nation-eating insects. And we strut around like so many prize barnyard roosters, proclaiming our invincibility --- our infallibility. We have become the world's best (worst) at destroying ourselves, spreading our tail feathers all the while --- too proud, too greedy, too selfish to sit down, look at ourselves, and for once, allow the term --- "UNITED" --- to truly mean something more than just a word we engrave on our precious money. But no. Even if it might purchase the lives of those most vulnerable --- those most innocent --- we turn our collective backs to swelling rivers of red. Instead of wallowing in overblown pride, we should be hiding our faces in utter shame. America the beautiful? One nation under God? All men created equal? REALLY? We deceive ourselves. TRUTH is, we excel in something different. We have become masters of our own pride-filled BLINDNESS.

· · · · ·

Remove CHARACTER from the leadership equation, and no amount of policy making skill can fill the void.

· · · · ·

If you have ever held a job, you have probably been on one end or the other of one of those "Evaluation/Performance" documents. They come in a huge variety of flavors and deal with things like promptness, dependability, attitude, ability to get along with peers, and other traits --- you know the deal. If you manage to check off a bunch of those "good boxes," then you can feel more secure in your position --- less threat of being shown the door. Falsify these forms, and everyone in the organization, no matter the arena, will ultimately suffer. This is true in the world of business, education, sports/entertainment --- everywhere. Oddly (or maybe not so oddly), rules and guidelines are violated most often (and cause the most damage) in the one arena that shouldn't tolerate such deceit

--- politics. But then, politics seems to work its way into all the other arenas anyway, doesn't it?

. . . . .

Perhaps we have forgotten the critical role INTEGRITY plays in a functioning democracy.

. . . . .

I played three sports in high school and two in college. Most people might think you have to be pretty tough to do that. Yet, I look at the photos of those little ones. They keep showing them, and those of the teacher and her husband --- both victims of this tragedy --- and I can't stop the tears. The emotions just well up in my chest, and I can't stop them. And I know this place; I've been here before.

. . . . .

"Get up, brush yourself off, and get back in there!" "Take one for the team!" Or (my all-time favorite): "Shake your head and spit!" Back in the day, coaches used to say some "odd" things, especially when you got hurt during competition –"got dinged", "got his bell rung" --- you know what I'm talking about. Do they still say such things? You have to be TOUGH to get back up and stay in the game with all the blows we're taking these days --- covid, mass shootings, climate change, economy, politics! SHAKE YOUR HEAD AND SPIT!

· · · · ·

With the price of eggs these days, you'd think they were laid by eagles.

· · · · ·

Republican-Democrat, Black-White, Arab-Jew, Catholic-Protestant, Native-Immigrant, Russian-Ukrainian, rich-poor, tall-short, thick-thin......I am so tired.

· · · · ·

Perhaps you have seen (felt) the emotional impact of a military funeral. A fallen American, no matter the age, is laid to rest with considerable pomp and ceremony --- a gun salute, the haunting sound of "Taps" played off in the distance, the very precise folding of the flag, and the dignified presentation of that flag to a widowed spouse or family member. Those at Arlington are particularly impressive and deeply moving. We will forever honor our fallen. No matter how you may feel about Russia or Russians right now, imagine the mothers, families, and friends of the tens of thousands of Russian soldiers who will never know what happened to their military family members, or friends --- never. General Sherman was right when he said, "War is hell." Why? Have you ever heard William Tecumseh Sherman's quote in its entirety? "IT IS ONLY THOSE WHO HAVE NEITHER FIRED A SHOT NOR HEARD THE SHRIEKS AND GROANS OF THE WOUNDED WHO CRY ALOUD FOR BLOOD, MORE VENGEANCE, MORE DESOLATION. WAR IS HELL." No matter on which side you fight, in war, there can be no winners.

· · · · ·

Without forgiveness, there is only vengeance.

· · · · ·

If our two major (and minor) political parties have taken everything we ALL know is "right," and DIVIDED it among themselves, it GUARANTEES perpetual disagreement because any one of them can make at least one valid point during any discussion regarding their overall views. I think THAT is at the core of why we see so much NEGATIVITY in political campaigns. No matter who's running, stick with what we ALL know is best for ALL citizens. Since opinions will always vary (as far as what's "right") COMPROMISE is essential. Maybe I over-simplify things too much. Maybe I should avoid all this political talk and just go fishing.

· · · · ·

Frustration is a good thing. Most likely, you are frustrated right now (and have been for some time) --- with HATRED. Everywhere you look these days (here and around the world), it finds a way to rear its ugly, Medusa head. Kindness shouldn't be restricted to holidays.

· · · · ·

"Senzeni Na?": "What have we done to deserve this strife?"

· · · · ·

"Sohlangana." : "We shall meet again in heaven."

--- South African apartheid folksong.

· · · · ·

Politicians and the media are forever flooding the airwaves with allegations and accusations about this and that --- who's doing what to whom, and who's getting what done (or not). As a result, these two very influential forces obligate their listeners to do research in order to confirm the accuracy of what they say (though much of what is touted as fact these days is, itself, often tainted). Too often, those who fail to fact-check thoroughly end up being the "sheep" that we hear so much about --- led around by the nose, and deceived by markets flooded with unprincipled individuals. In the end, those who, for whatever reason, fail (or refuse) to validate claims that may "appear" to be true, valid, and logical sometimes make victims of themselves. How many terms, including slang, appear in nearly every language that mean to trick or deceive? Honesty and integrity must really mean something.

· · · · ·

DECEPTION: making someone believe something that isn't true. In that regard, the world is truly gifted. It forever tries to convince you that there is actually such a thing as an AVERAGE person.

· · · · ·

When I think about the variety of PEOPLES who populate this earth, I am amazed. The incredible diversity in our nation alone is mind-boggling! Think of a state --- any state --- then imagine people from several different cultures who reside there. It's not difficult at all --- from Maine to Arizona, from Washington to Florida --- any and all the states in between: Kansas, Minnesota, Colorado, Maryland, Texas, just to name a few. Imagine all those people from all those places, then imagine life if those were the types of people running our cities, states, the entire country. Now consider a GLOBAL view --- the rice farmer outside of Hanoi, the cab driver in New Delhi, the family that runs the seafood market in Santiago, the owner of the small restaurant in Paris, the teacher in Nairobi. If the types of people you thought of were the ones running things, most likely, nobody would need a military. We've really gotten off-track, haven't we?

. . . . .

As we witness repeated (rising?) cases of corruption, perversion --- tragedy of every description --- I must confess that I've grown weary of hearing the statement, "This is not us." Apparently, this IS us!

. . . . .

It seems "SHAMELESS" is the latest virtue, doesn't it?

. . . . .

Some of us are old enough to remember when the party of the sitting president didn't really matter very much when it came to selecting candidates for the Supreme Court.

. . . . .

Even in the face of grave danger, it is still best to not be so easily frightened.

. . . . .

People everywhere cherish FREEDOM. That's why prisons have forever been considered "severe punishment." Yet, when you consider this current plague of mass shootings, there must be a growing number of people who do not value freedom, or their very lives, at all.

• • • • •

Is there any such thing as a "perfect law?" Imperfect people create imperfect rules, so there simply can't be any such animal. Welfare helps a lot of legitimately needy people, but some will abuse it. Taxes, as much as we hate them, are essential in funding many programs, but some will always find ways to evade paying their share. This is true of ANY policy we create. "Slam dunks" are rare. Gun rights are certainly among the most controversial. They beg one crucial process --- ARBITRATION. Will we remain too stubborn --- too proud? For the sake of everyone, we had better sit down and TALK so we can come up with some new, effective ideas. We have passenger service on rockets to outer space, for crying out loud! Pointing angry fingers at each other is not getting the job done. While we are throwing chairs and kicking the dog, innocent people (we're losing count) are dying.

• • • • •

Certainly, since nine-eleven, the mere mention of "terrorism" has drawn the immediate attention of every American. We relentlessly beat the bushes (all over the world) to root out the perpetrators but never bothered to look in our own backyard.

. . . . .

FINDERS KEEPERS: These days, it seems the whole world is in disarray. In all the turmoil, the problems appear to far outnumber the problem-solvers, mostly because we have lost the desire to include one key, fundamental factor in our efforts --- TRUTH. As a result, stress levels are elevated as never before. Every day, everybody has to deal with lies, deceit, scams, and hacks --- being bamboozled at every turn, a snake under every bush. Have you noticed how many words there are, in every language, that mean to get "tricked" or "fooled?" People have always had a problem with truth, and these days, they seem to have added a strong tendency to ignore or deny it. When we pull back the covers and expose the real culprit behind today's most volatile issues, the total disregard for truth is revealed, smiling, and lying (literally) under the mattress. The failure to keep it foremost in all that we do is a main reason why the other half of that little childhood phrase was coined in the first place: LOSERS WEEPERS --- that part, surely as true as the first.

· · · · ·

During these inflationary times, they've actually been with us for a while, you've no doubt noticed how many of the products you use have shrunk in size/volume even as their prices have risen. That huge "dimple" in the bottom of those juice jugs has caught your attention, and you're paying for a lot more needless packaging these days too! How many times have you cursed those clear plastic containers as you desperately tried to get to those batteries or that shaver and blades, even with your best scissors? They package the daylights out of simple stuff, but "sensitive" items like electronics (printer cartridges?) require a separate instruction manual, in four languages. Here's a simple but sneaky one. Once upon a time, bars of soap were much larger. For cryin' out loud, you once had to break a bar of Ivory soap in half. (Does it still float?) Lifebuoy, Zest (who thought of those names?) were not only much larger, but one bar used to last for weeks. Two face washings with a modern bar of Dove (one-quarter cleansing cream and all), and it's time for another one. They dissolve faster than Alka-Seltzer! Is that by design? And what about your car? They manufacture them so YOU can't repair even simple stuff anymore. "Computer modules" run everything. Seen a spark plug lately? You have to be an automotive engineer just to FIND them! Cars are reliable 'til you make the last payment. But towing is covered in your insurance premiums, but let's not even get into geckos and emus. Have you looked under the hood of a late-model car recently? They've encased everything in tamper-proof (YOU-proof) compartments. Forget about those jumper cables! And with your new electric pick-up, who needs a home generator? Mechanic school anyone? Do-It-Yourself (DIY) these days only applies when you go to the bathroom.

· · · · ·

The economy, crime, discrimination, immigration, conspiracy theories galore: Fear is obviously a powerful tool. Has it ever been more extensively manipulated against its most effective countermeasures --- COURAGE, FAITH, HOPE? It must not be allowed to win.

· · · · ·

Many today might find it difficult to believe television commercials for cigarettes and cigars were once quite common, but advertisements for alcohol and prescription drugs were prohibited.

· · · · ·

Watching television, social media, or whatever source of world news and events, it's easy to be pessimistic, even depressed. It seems human beings, worldwide, are behaving more and more like monsters. However, if you take the time to look under the covers, you'll discover there are far more who behave like angels, and you can choose the role you wish to play. It's the best way to counter that huge, dark wave. There are ALWAYS more beautiful hearts. Join them, and don't be discouraged. In the midst of the worst storms, even "little old you" can make a positive, significant difference.

· · · · ·

Don't want to watch the news anymore, do you? It's understandable. These are perfect times to have your own quiet place --- park, beach, patio. Visit as often as necessary; it's okay. Things will get better.

· · · · ·

For as long as I've been around, I am still amazed at just how powerful a force simple GREED can be on the human psyche.

· · · · ·

POLITICAL OPINION: I think it is shameful --- a disgrace --- how our nation has made a political tennis ball out of the right to vote. There are those on one hand who proclaim the sacred nature of our Constitution --- "Stars and Stripes Forever!"--- while on the other, appear eager to disrupt --- indeed, dismantle --- the very mechanism that makes a democracy a democracy. I have seen politicians stoop mighty low in my years, but this ranks right up there (down there) with that blatant and violent miscarriage of freedom that took place last January 6th. Some to this day still try to justify even that. Rant over.

. . . . .

Day after day, we hear story after story of Ukrainians demonstrating incredible courage against the seemingly overwhelming forces of the Russian Federation. And yet, on the home front, day after day, we hear story after story of politicians demonstrating incredible cowardice in fear of the seemingly overwhelming forces of the American voter.

. . . . .

Whether you know or believe the story of the Garden of Eden or not, one thing holds true. Satan never actually accused God of being "wrong." He simply PLANTED DOUBT in the minds of Adam and Eve about God's motives being "right." Even today, it is an incredibly powerful and effective tactic. Undermine the credibility of those who are ordinarily considered most credible.

. . . . .

A 6-yr.-old bringing a gun to school and actually shooting his teacher is, yet another, wake-up call. Some of us remember when one of the most serious offenses committed in the classroom was chewing gum.

• • • • •

Myth, legend, fable, tale, folklore, theory --- lots of terms that mean the same thing. When people don't know the facts, they MAKE UP stuff!

• • • • •

"Smoke and mirrors", "pull the wool over your eyes", "muddy the waters" --- there are countless ways to describe the ever-popular process of deceiving others. How can so many be so easily victimized by it? Each of us is given eyes with which to see, ears with which to hear, and a brain with which to think/reason. It's not really as difficult to determine what is just and unjust in this world (as many are led to believe). Yet, they choose to remove their glasses, plug their ears, give up on thinking/reasoning and allow themselves to be led by unscrupulous individuals who claim to have perfect vision, hearing, and reasoning skills. The "fight for right" will forever be a huge struggle.

• • • • •

Isn't it interesting how easily hatred and selfishness can cause people to sacrifice everything, including their lives, as can love and selflessness?

· · · · ·

These days, I sure wish "reeling" only referred to fishing.

· · · · ·

There is good reason why most of the highest-ranking military officers actually hate war. They know the horrors better than most. A news commentator said recently that the longer this conflict between Russia and Ukraine goes on, the greater the "advantage" is to Russia because of the greater size of their war-making machine. But recent developments have opened a few eyes. The Ukrainians are fierce fighters. Adequately supplied, they have proven themselves willing and capable of defending their own homeland. You can see it even in the eyes of their oldest citizens. At whatever cost, they have made it obvious that they are NOT going to quit. But Russia, too, has already paid a terrible price in men and equipment, including 9 of their generals. You witness the terrible suffering that is war, and are appalled that it's really all about satisfying one --- JUST ONE --- overinflated ego. How many times must THAT scenario be replayed --- those same lessons be taught --- before we realize there are no winners in wars?

· · · · ·

When a majority of the people believe a certain way ---
support certain ideas --- and their wishes are either ignored
or denied, then their leaders are negligent. Therein lies the
critical significance of ELECTIONS.

· · · · ·

PERSPECTIVE (point of view): the ability to express it is
basic --- freedom of speech at its purest. Someone observes
an item, or considers an issue, then shares his conclusions.
He is free to see and think as he chooses, but that's where
one key element --- TRUTH --- enters the equation. Truth
implies correctness and propriety, but from whose
perspective? Who decides what's "right?" Inaccuracy
complicates and confuses because people tend to make of
things what they choose, then present them as truth. But if
truth IS truth (there can only be one), then everything else,
by default, must be false. Humans routinely deceive
themselves. Myth, legend, lore, tale, fable, etc. have played
a key role in every culture. However, they do not require
fact, truth, or evidence. The denial of fact invites untested,
twisted --- even perverse --- perspectives and those are often
presented as truth based primarily on how fervently they are
believed. That is the essence of cults. That's why, today, we
are awash in them.

· · · · ·

The more information you learn about a topic, the more options available to choose from concerning it. The more options there are to choose from, the greater the chances of making sound, informed decisions. It changes the landscape when people "know better" (better know). Education is an amoeba, constantly changing, but it's not the bogeyman that many these days want to make it. Young people are not puppets led around by master puppeteers. EDUCATION says, "Here's what's out there. What do YOU think?" Of course, there are limitations, but when a nation decides to criticize or otherwise impede that message, then that nation automatically places its future --- its most valuable natural resource --- on very thin ice. (JMHO)

· · · · ·

There is no shortage of critics of this nation and/or its leadership, but you won't find many who don't experience some level of relief/joy when the wheels touch down from even the most wonderful trip abroad.

· · · · ·

A common buzzword these days: UNPRECEDENTED. It can conjure demons --- all the NEGATIVITY that we witness in the world today, but it should also conjure POSITIVITY --- countermeasures that help inspire survivability and hopes of "thrivability."

····

These days especially, we so often hear/mention idyllic terms like justice, equality, human rights, and such, but some routinely make statements that openly deny those basic freedoms to certain portions of the population --- their meaning, often "cloaked" in nebulous, worn-out terminologies. The depth of the deception is truly profound, or, deep down inside, do they really "know?" Reconciliation, if it happens at all, will be a long, interesting struggle.

····

Feeling wrobbed of wrights, caught between a wrock and a hard place, fearing a day of wreckoning is at hand? Maybe mankind is not as good at running the world as he has phorever convinced himself.

····

If you are one of the many who choose to debate the current political climate in this country, remember it's perfectly fine to use a tight end as your quarterback, or to scout the opposing team before an upcoming contest, BUT you may not use your football bat or your soccer racquet in the game and expect the officials to simply turn a blind eye. The rules are there for a reason. Without them, you can't know what game you're playing.

· · · · ·

Campaign/election results ultimately say as much, or more, about the citizenry/character of a nation as they do about its candidates/nominees.

· · · · ·

Despite all that you see in this life, it still seems inappropriate to place the word "only" before "human."

· · · · ·

The longer I live, the more I realize our national colors are really red, white, and GREEN.

· · · · ·

Material wealth is but the steppingstone to that which most easily seduces mankind --- POWER.

· · · · ·

REPROBATE: The word sounds like something having to do with taxes, or perhaps inheritance, however, its meaning is quite different. While it can mean "morally depraved," it can also mean "rejected by God and beyond hope of salvation." My grandmother used to say, "Some folks just ain't gon' do right." These are interesting times.

· · · · ·

Peace and happiness are soulmates. It is a mistake to fill the void from their absence with politics.

· · · · ·

It is amazing, and disappointing, how many people are afraid to confront the limits of their own thinking.

· · · · ·

Especially these days, it seems "politics" should be spelled with a "K."

· · · · ·

The urge (obsession?) to control others is powerful, widespread, and goes unrecognized far more often than cases of drug abuse.

· · · · ·

More than anything, dictators, tyrants, autocrats --- "bullies" of all types --- fear EDUCATION. It is far easier to control the minds of the ignorant than it is the learned. That's why their control tactics often include exiling scholars, imprisoning dissidents, banning books, and forbidding the study of history --- all those things that give people a better, clearer understanding of themselves and their own identities.

· · · · ·

What is this incessant obsession that mankind has with CONQUERING? Go back as far in history as you like. One group of human beings is forever trying to "conquer" others. PEACE is truly a rare commodity. If history means anything, it looks like we're in for at least a few more days of unrest --- conflict.

· · · · ·

We do not wish sadness upon anyone, but it is particularly heartbreaking when victims of tragedy are kids --- ANY kids --- especially when so much sorrow is preventable. Sad tears are always bitter, but those --- particularly so. Despite all that we know about disease, famine, war, and carelessness, young lives are erased before they have the chance to even make their mark. "Knowing" does not necessarily mean "learning," does it?

· · · · ·

I could spend the rest of my life lamenting the many evil things I've seen human beings do, but I'd much rather focus on all the wonderful things I've been blessed to see them do --- some, bona fide miracles. Those are the things that have fed my convictions and strengthened my determination to be the best I can be --- far from perfect, yet better than I would ever have otherwise been.

. . . . .

People who love people don't depend on material wealth to find peace and happiness. Their treasure lies in their relationships with others. Those we call "haters" blindly worship material gain, place their "faith" in it, and never, ever find true satisfaction, happiness, or peace. Pity them.

. . . . .

I have kissed warm faces; I have shaken strong hands --- hugged close enough to feel hearts beat. But I have also touched faces and hands that were cold and still --- stroked muscles that I knew would forever remain motionless. Properly viewed, such experiences enhance life, and in powerful ways, move us to do better during our stay here.

. . . . .

It has been said: "The only thing necessary for evil to triumph is for good men to do nothing."- Edmund Burke. It's interesting how evil spreads much faster than good --- almost as if it has a life of its own. Humans are naturally better together, and yet, evil (in an amazing variety of ways) manages to drive wedges between people. As a result, everyone ultimately suffers, and everyone suffers ultimately. Is this a statement about human nature, where evil is innate, and good must be taught?

. . . . .

Why such greed? In the eyes of some, ultimate WEALTH equals ultimate POWER. You just can't factor MONEY out of the equation, can you?

. . . . .

How many instances can you cite in history where people (usually in tears) lamented, "They took the children?" Cruelty, in all its many forms, is alive and well (has forever been, it seems). Be kind.

. . . . .

Even if you were born as recently as the turn of the century, you have witnessed amazing CHANGES in this world --- everywhere. Think about the meaning of the word "security" now. Once upon a time, it was one of the most BORING jobs anybody could ever work. And now...whoa!

. . . . .

It sounds rather gruesome, but the old saying, "You must cut the head off the snake" is true. Once done, the tail may move for a while, but eventually, even that will stop.

"...Live in peace with one another. And we urge you, bretheren, admonish the unruly, encourage the fainthearted, help the weak, and be patient with all men. See that no one repays another with evil for evil, but always seek after that which is good for one another and for all men." 1 Thessalonians 5: 13-15   Who can question the wisdom of these words? People SAY they believe what scripture says, but many do not LIVE it. Continue to share the truth anyway. Eventually, some will listen.

· · · · ·

Regarding this recent assassination attempt, many are asking themselves, "How has it come to this?" --- as if it's something new. This great country of ours has ALWAYS been politically violent. Stop and think about it. Change? It's up to us, U.S.

· · · · ·

The world has far too much pain and suffering already for me to do anything to add to it.

· · · · ·

JMHO again --- long post, sorry: Part of the intro to the old, old TV Superman program (circa 1960's starring George

Reeves) went this way, "...Superman, who can change the course of mighty rivers, bend steel in his bare hands and who, disguised as Clark Kent --- mild-mannered reporter for a great metropolitan newspaper --- fights a never-ending battle for TRUTH, JUSTICE, AND THE AMERICAN WAY" (emphasis mine). This Juneteenth, beyond simply being "released to roam about," what did "emancipation" really mean to former slaves? The "40 acres and a mule" thing was torpedoed even before they were invented. (Oh, what MIGHT have happened if...!) Andrew Johnson was known for his alcoholism problem and his public use of the "N" word. And though he was the first U.S. president to be impeached, his decision to fire those torpedoes was upheld. Not surprisingly, he nixed the idea of slaves being landowners. That program was actually started, but Johnson decided it was better to return the land to the slave owners. Who should know that (among so many other historical facts)? EVERY American! To not know can be devastating. Our history does prove THAT. It is a myth that enlightenment about America's Black (or any other) history inspires/generates racial hatred. NOT teaching ALL of history is the ultimate UNtruth. In fact, surveys reveal the vast majority of Black people, when asked if they hate white people because of atrocities their ancestors committed, say "NO." However, most are equally quick to add that they ARE, in fact, deeply angered by the fact that they were never told "the TRUTH, the whole TRUTH, and nothing but the

TRUTH." After all, partial truth is, by default, just another deception --- a lie of "omission." Ironically, Jesus is quoted as saying, "I am the way, the TRUTH (emphasis mine), and the life..." --- John 14: 6. (Truth MUST be powerful stuff.) Even Superman was dedicated to finding it --- fighting for it. However, those dedicated to finding TRUTH must first begin with a thorough, honest examination of SELF.

· · · · ·

When a nation, for whatever reason, decides to go to war, it has also decided that the sacrifice of its most precious (priceless) resource --- ITS YOUTH --- is worth the cause.

· · · · ·

Throughout human history, imagine the amount of pain, suffering, and death that have occurred simply because one group of individuals decided it was somehow "better" than another.

· · · · ·

Those devastating events of life can really bring you down. Watch the news, and the burdens get even tougher to bear. Mere survival becomes a struggle, and the phrase, "going to hell in a handbasket" takes on new meaning. During downtimes, it's good --- therapeutic --- to remember the GREAT PEOPLE you have in your life. It's easy to forget how many, but even a chosen few can help you navigate some of the deepest, darkest waters --- rough seas that life never seems to run out of.

· · · · ·

Never have there been more people, running down their own streets, each totally convinced he is the only one headed in the right direction.

AGING

A Mixed Blessing

The older I get, the more I realize how, after a certain age, people begin to disappear.

· · · · ·

When I was a little guy, I wondered what old folks think about so much. They sit there on their porches, in their Lazy-boy rocker recliners, on park benches --- even in the busiest environments --- just staring. During most of their waking hours, I believe old people play and replay old movies in their minds. Recently, more and more, I've been enjoying a few old classics myself.

· · · · ·

I used to wonder what it was that made old people so bold. They tend to speak their minds --- act with utter impunity--- while younger people tend to simply make more noise. Older people have a "What are you gonna do to me" --- "Ain't got much to lose no how" attitude --- often the result of many years of experience - WISDOM. From just another senior citizen (still sounds funny to use that term in reference to myself): be wary of those who preach the suppression of the WHOLE truth. They prefer to ignore it, or otherwise sweep it under the rug, in an incredible variety of ways. Poisons can sometimes be flushed out by bloodletting.

. . . . .

When I walk past people at building entrances and in parking lots, I'm finding it interesting to have them call me "Sir." For a long time, I covered my gray head with a ball cap. Then my mustache was giving me away. The N-95 mask helped a lot there 'til my EYEBROWS decided to get into the act!

. . . . .

"In the race of life, time ALWAYS has the better kick."

. . . . .

Those who are blessed enough to work/live long enough soon realize that "retirement" is not what they thought. Of course, there is more time for "personal gratifications" --- long-awaited trips to exotic destinations, and not having to wait 'til the weekend or summertime to grab a moment of relaxation --- dinner at a special restaurant or even an unplanned nap. Indeed, it doesn't take very long for rookie retirees to realize there is (still) much work to be done. It (the work) somehow finds them. The difference lies mainly in the ability to choose AGENDA and PACE. That extra bit of "control" is where the joy of retirement truly lies.

· · · · ·

Years after he retired, I watched my father's countenance change. He seemed more distant --- reflective. As he saw the sun slowly set on his own life, he watched it set on many of his dear friends and loved ones. I watched as he watched. These days, I am there; I understand.

· · · · ·

There is this huge, strange sense of relief now, finally. So many I know now understand. They see --- horrified and bewildered. I was born in the FIFTIES! Can you even begin to imagine?

· · · · ·

Unfortunately, "FR" has appeared in front of the modifier that once described me perfectly --- "AGILE."

· · · · ·

I went fishing yesterday --- more to contemplate things than to catch anything. As I sat there patiently, the rod tip bent over more than ninety degrees. A big one had taken one of my baits. Excited, I tried to jump up and grab the rod to reel in "the big one," AND FELL FLAT ON MY FACE --- hurt one knee, two fingers, and bumped my forehead on the ground, losing my glasses. My legs used to be so strong. Now, they were telling me that I need to warn them first if I'm going to be making any sudden moves. They need time to prepare. The message was simple (clear): "We're sorry, but we weren't ready." To top it off, the fish got away, probably laughing. Birthdays mean aging, and aging means the loss of some abilities, but I wasn't yet ready to accept standing up as one of them. Getting older also means learning to laugh at the dumb stuff you're GOING to do, then being willing to share openly what a clutz you can be! If I do say so myself, I've gotten good at it.

· · · · ·

I've been a guy all my life (surprise, surprise). Culturally, I've been taught to "act" like a guy. That means a zillion things --- too many, in fact, to detail here. Among them, however, is this conscious/subconscious attitude, for that's really all it is, to demean women --- to make them feel somehow "less than." It didn't work. I've been black all my life (surprise, surprise). Culturally, I've been taught to "act" black. That means a zillion things --- too many, in fact, to detail here. Among them, however, is this conscious/subconscious attitude, for that's all it really is, that I should feel demeaned --- somehow "less than." It didn't work. Now that I can incorporate that magical, 3-ingredient recipe into my life --- OLD, BLACK, GUY--- it occurs to me that many, simply through a false elevation of self, have cheated themselves out of unspeakable blessing --- untold treasures. We have come far, but we still have far to go. Only now are we beginning to realize. Better late than never, they say, but what if...?

• • • • •

Most of us have watched little ones at play alone --- interesting because their little imaginations are so alive. They invent friends, villains --- faraway places. With t-shirts tied securely around little necks, they become superheroes. Don't you just love the voices? They have specially selected, magical, secret places: under the stairway, in the attic, under the bed, or some fort carefully constructed in an unused part of the house or a treehouse in the backyard. Then, just like that, you're cheering for them at their graduation. Goes fast, doesn't it?

• • • • •

One of the greatest, most unsung blessings of being "older" is simply watching your own kids' kids, and all your loved ones' (friends, family members --- students, athletes, colleagues) kids' kids enjoy holidays like this! Christmas blessings to you all!

• • • • •

Some of you will remember when you were younger, and you used to see someone's, usually a grandparent's, PILLBOX (wherever they stored it). They came in a multitude of sizes and colors --- M-T-W-T-F-S-S. (I never thought about it before, but in Spanish, those letters would be L-M-M-J-V-S-D. Some of you are thinking about even more languages right now, aren't you?) Remember back then how you convinced yourself you'd NEVER have to take all those colorful pills, capsules, caplets, and these days, all those GUMMY SUPPLEMENTS? Your body USED to produce sufficient quantities of all that stuff --- calcium, potassium, iron --- its own WD-40! Well, now you know --- grocery stores aren't the only places with shortages. When you get right down to it though, gray hair, wrinkles, and creaky joints ain't so bad, after all, as they say, "it beats the alternative!" Then again, would you be willing to do it all again?

• • • • •

Just a thought: Counting from the day you took your first step, if you could calculate the TOTAL DISTANCE you have covered in your life, walking and EVERY other mode of transportation, just how far would you have traveled? Just the total travel to and from SCHOOL(S) would be impressive, huh? Just how much have you LEARNED? Now, consider how well you've APPLIED all that you have learned. If your life were a classroom (as indeed it is), what grade would you give yourself?

．．．．．

PERSONAL: As a former athlete, I remember training --- competing until I had absolutely nothing left. Pedal to the metal 'til I ran out of gas --- out of fumes. It's what good teammates are supposed to do, right? I wanted to be a good teammate. As an educator and a coach, I remember teaching and coaching, giving until I had absolutely nothing left. Pedal to the metal 'til I ran out of gas --- out of fumes. While in college, I was an exchange student (Madrid). One day, I got into a fight with another exchange student (from Norway). We both lived with the same family. The fight? Of all things, he repeatedly said bad things about the USA. (The VietNam War was still raging.) I'm not proud of it, but I beat him up pretty good/bad. He kept saying those things and one day, I just ran out of gas --- out of fumes. We broke the senora's lamp, but she didn't mind very much; she didn't like him either. I never felt so red, white, and blue. I got tired of him saying those things. Today, I'm a lot older --- and maybe a bit wiser. I probably wouldn't make a good teammate, teacher, coach, exchange student, or fighter today, I'm too tired. I've run out of gas yet again. This time, because of the way I see so many people behaving. I'm frustrated not as much with the huge challenges of our times, but also with HOW WE TREAT EACH OTHER --- a lesson I learned from a Norwegian, of all people. It occurs to me that I've never really been THIS tired of anything. I've changed. I probably won't be visiting Oslo any time soon, but I've never gotten tired of fishing.

· · · · ·

Some remember when power windows and power steering were luxury options on new cars. And the turn signal lever did nothing more than signal your intention to make a turn. Steering wheels, four tires (and sometimes a hood ornament) were standard though.

· · · · ·

Without going into a lot of detail, I can say old bodies definitely get "noisier."

· · · · ·

It's easy to see/understand how human beings, especially the youngest, go through "stages," but when you think about it, stages are perpetual --- endless, for all of us. You're thinking of a dozen or so right now.

· · · · ·

Because the story doesn't end with your passing, what you do now, while you have the chance, means EVERYTHING. The word is not mentioned nearly enough, but LEGACY is so important.

· · · · ·

Time is precious --- limited. Don't waste it. Two weeks ago, it was April. You were still looking forward to proms, graduations, and summer vacations. You told yourself you had time. July Fourth is tomorrow. Whatever it is, better to get it done now.

· · · · ·

Aging is a fascinating process. From the beginning, you learn it is best to pay attention to everything going on around you. That way, the learning never stops, important in helping you choose the right path in that all-important quest for self-identity. When (if) you manage to clear that huge hurdle, you recognize the difference between intelligence and wisdom --- success and significance. With a clearer sense of purpose, goals are set. You learn that youth comes and goes all too quickly, and it's true, "Beauty is only skin-deep." Wisdom teaches you that beauty lies in the heart --- in a willingness to LOVE and to pursue LOVE for the treasure that it is. Then, as your physical eyes dim, your spiritual eyes are opened. You are never again satisfied with the "status quo" because you can now recognize the depth and breadth of the wrong that goes on around you --- always. Time inevitably brings change, and you must change with it --- driven more than ever to do your part in making this world a better place. Finally, you can go to your rest because you should, understandably, be exhausted.

· · · · ·

One year is 25% of a 4-year-old's life, 4% of a 25-year-old's life, and 2% of a 50-year-old's life. 4-year-olds think of future days; 25-year-olds of future years, and 50-year-olds of past decades. Little wonder time seems to accelerate as we age.

· · · · ·

Somehow, you neglect to prepare yourself to be referred to as "that old dude."

· · · · ·

These days, I laugh when I hear the phrase, ". . .if you're over 40."

· · · · ·

Because young people are young people, each with little experience and yearning for significance --- to be somebody, they overlook the fact that their particular gift(s) may not require big stages and bright lights.

· · · · ·

Growing old can present far more than just "physical" challenges.

· · · · ·

The younger generation will have only read or heard about them, but some will remember Jackie Gleason, Lucille Ball, Red Skelton, Sammy Davis Jr., Dean Martin, Marion Anderson, James Brown, Bart Starr, Dwight D. Eisenhower, John F. Kennedy --- lots of famous people from the distant past. During their heyday, everyone knew them; they were household names. Today, they all have one thing in common. They are all gone. A line from a song, "If I Were King Of The Forest" (sung by the Cowardly Lion in "The Wizard of Oz") asks, "What have they got that I ain't got?" The answer is NOTHING, and if the endings are inevitable --- all destined to be the same --- then fame, fortune, and power must be grossly overrated. It's okay to admire the accomplishments of the famous, but we probably shouldn't envy them --- clamoring over autographs, trinkets, and souvenirs. To do so is like admitting they have done something that you never could. When your own day is done here, comparatively few will probably ever know, or care, that you ever existed. Your greatest goal in life should be simpler. You only need to help as many as you can (like birds) to fly. Accomplish that one goal, and you can know for sure that your life here meant something --- that it was more than just a "flash in the pan."

· · · · ·

Only recently, I've come to realize that 70 is not as far from 40 as I once thought.

· · · · ·

The older you get, the more you appreciate opening your eyes each morning. Family, friends, dawns, and sunsets are wonder-filled bonuses.

· · · · ·

People tell stories about getting old all the time, but there's an important fact that people should realize as they age. Your body WILL lie to you! Given just the right set of circumstances, say, there's a crowd of people watching, it will try to convince you that you can still do things that your common sense says you can't. Almost inevitably, your body will say, "You can still do that --- no problem," but your common sense chimes in and asks a couple of simple questions like: "Are you out of your ever-loving mind? Are your insurance premiums current?" It's best to listen to

THAT voice (your conscience). It knows that if you dare put that rickety, old bag of bones in gear before engaging your brain, feeble though that may be, the consequences could be painful. You foolishly think you can still clear a hurdle (it's just a low one) even though you regularly trip over small items on your bedroom floor --- a house slipper or a stray dust bunny. If you remain defiant, you old jock, you, your conscience may not argue. "Go ahead; just remember I told you." Only when you regain consciousness in the ambulance or hospital are you convinced that your body routinely lies to you! You ARE older and can't do even slightly risky stuff anymore. Old ex-athletes are particularly vulnerable; non-athletes, hold onto that beer and the tv remote.

· · · · ·

Successful or not, it is interesting how we grow up looking toward the future --- at what we PLAN to do. Then at some point, it varies, it reverses itself and we begin to look BACKWARD --- at what we've managed to get done. Ultimately, we must come to grips with how we've spent our time here on this earth --- Result: SATISFACTION or REGRET. In the end, what was the REAL WORTH of all you did?

· · · · ·

Only a minority of human beings have a thorough and accurate awareness of the concept of TIME. Yet, it totally controls our lives. Sadly, when that awareness becomes known, it is often too late.

· · · · ·

Gray or thinning hair (beards included), creaky joints, failing eyesight/hearing, an amazing array of braces --- knee, back, neck (but not teeth; those days --- like real teeth --- long gone), AARP subscriptions, a host of mental ailments, mostly memory loss, and that saving grace --- GRANDPARENTHOOD --- and these are descriptions of the STUDENTS and ATHLETES that I once taught and coached! So where does that leave ME?

· · · · ·

I just realized one of the greatest blessings of being old. I write a lot of stuff about a lot of stuff --- much of it, just a little _____(fill in the blank), BUT at my age, I don't worry much about what anybody decides to write on that blank. This is a whole 'nother kind of FREEDOM!

· · · · ·

OLD SAYING: "You scrape and pinch and sacrifice --- work like a dog your entire life to get to those 'greener pastures' --- and when you finally get there, you're too tired to climb the fence!" That is as it SHOULD be. Of the huge variety of CAREERS to choose from, many have sweated and toiled long enough (in 1 or more) and earned the right to graze, at long last, in those lush, green fields we call retirement. You gave it your all while you were there in those trenches. Every day you could --- season in, season out --- you added "dependable" to the discussion when others spoke of you. You were careful enough --- WISE enough, however --- to remember to take time to regularly recharge your batteries. After all, marathoners ALWAYS have regular "rehydration stations." Good reputations mean so much, and when the journey comes to an end (as it inevitably must), there will be no need for any regrets. You pushed a little harder, a little longer, and most important, OTHERS benefited because you did. If those were priorities, then career choice shouldn't matter very much. You learned the most critical lesson of all --- the difference between success and significance. Now, whether it's alfalfa, bermuda, or some "exotic," ENJOY! You've earned the right to choose!

· · · · ·

Now that I'm just a little older, my strength and sense of balance are not what they used to be. Once upon a time, I could accidentally knock a container off a table and catch it before it hit the floor. Reflexes were on point! Now I try,and usually fail, to get my foot out of the way before the container crashes on it. At my age, it's good to learn another essential skill --- HOW TO FALL --- gracefully. After a while, you don't really care who sees you take a spill as long as nobody feels the need to call 911. I give finesse to "tuck and roll." Like a freshly trimmed log, in slow motion, I've learned to "round those edges" so I don't break anything. If someone sees me take a spill, I don't care if they laugh, but I've gotten so good, I don't expect laughter; I expect APPLAUSE! Thank you, thank you!

· · · · ·

Most likely, you've had a little experience with that classic "stubborn little kid." You've seen them strike the pose in supermarkets, on the playground, in their crib --- squinty little eyes, little pursed lips, little arms folded across little chests, little feet firmly planted --- uninvited behaviors that can appear quite suddenly, with NO formal instruction whatsoever, and all within just a few MONTHS of graduation to solid foods! Of course, teens can be impressive too when it comes to stubbornness. I know you're thinking of other, far more "colorful" modifiers, I can hear the amens! They say they'll starve themselves, run away, or report parents, teachers, coaches, any authority figure, to the police (or any OTHER authority figure) if they are not allowed to "go Burger King" --- have it THEIR way. Look around you. There are an awful lot of 30, 40, 50, 60, and even 70-year-old TODDLERS and TEENAGERS running around these days! Have you noticed?

· · · · ·

I just realized my very first students have children who have children who have children. My life sure must have been fun; I can't even remember where it went! Does it really go that fast, or has my memory really gotten that bad?

If you really want to know what this life is all about --- all that truly matters during your fleeting stay here – so many spend their entire lives searching --- simply sit and have a chat with someone who is staring, or has stared ETERNITY in the face --- profound.

· · · · ·

I don't claim to be anybody special, but I love just boppin' around, doing what old dudes do --- goin' to the grocery store to buy bread, my favorite ice cream, and wondering what people think when they see me. If they don't know me, then they can't possibly see me either --- makes me feel a little like a (Black) Clark Kent. There is a 100% chance that I will be misidentified --- 100% DIFFERENT from who they THINK I am. My disguises are quite effective --- bifocals, knee brace, sweatpants, orthopedic shoes. I find entertainment wherever, whenever, and however I can, but

I must remember the "K-I-S-S Principle" --- nothing stressful or strenuous.

· · · · ·

Few people openly discuss it, but something powerful (spiritual? magical?) happens when (if) you reach that proverbial age of "3 score and 10." Of course, there are the usual physical issues (no details necessary; too many to list anyway), but the less obvious, mental ones are amazing! It's ironic that it's when your eyesight begins to fade that you really begin to see! Sadly, that's also when people consider you so old that you're not worth listening to and it's then that you have so many pertinent things to say. The gray hair and wrinkles do something to their sense of appreciation of time and experience, I guess. Interestingly, if you pay close enough attention, there will be other "signals." Very powerful, mostly unexpected "rewards of life" begin to appear, and you can never figure out the timing of their delivery. They may include everything from reconnects with long, lost friends, to surprise material gain. Most important is a realization that, unconsciously, you gain the most precious gift of all --- WISDOM.

· · · · ·

Okay, so I will cease and desist discussing the "can't do anymore" stuff that comes with aging, and point out a truly amazing, valuable skill that also comes with the years. Arguably, the most critical one is the ability to discern, detect, determine, differentiate, discriminate, distinguish, and divine. (All those D's remind me of my report card.) One of the funniest ironies in life is that your eyesight only becomes 20/20 when your eyes start to go bad.

· · · · ·

Everyone gets a brand-new vehicle. The intent is to take care of it so it will last a "decent" number of years. For a number of reasons, and despite our best efforts, that number often varies greatly. It is wise to get regular tune-ups. Certain parts are subject to greater amounts of wear and tear. Safety and longevity go hand in hand. It pays to fill up with quality fuels, check and change fluid levels, and kick the tires every now and again. Improperly inflated tires can silently cause fuel waste, loss of mileage --- disaster. Because there are so many other vehicles on the road, safety means always keeping an eye out for them. The careless and the reckless can cause untimely visits to the repair shop (or worse) --- expensive and no fun. While some take meticulous care of their vehicles; others don't. Some keep their paint shining like glass, while some paint jobs fall victim to rust and corrosion. Some engines purr like kittens; others creak and clank like old mill wheels. With sport, compact, luxury, sport utility, or truck, the same rules apply.

Take care of them and they'll take care of you. Abuse them --- fail to perform proper maintenance --- and problems, unhappy (even tragic) results can occur. All vehicles, even motorcycles, are precious and worth your time and care. It all begins, and ends, with how you see and treat your vehicle. In truth, you really only get ONE new one. By the way, how many miles do you have on YOUR odometer? ***To be clear, this piece is NOT about automobiles.

· · · · ·

Nearly every hair on my head is white. Younger people, even ladies, hold doors for me, and people almost always say, "yes sir or no sir." Question: At what age do people consider THEMSELVES "elderly?" I still FEEL like I look thirty-six, but I guess not. In my wallet, I always keep my driver's license facedown.

· · · · ·

Don't know if it's a thing for older folks or not, but did you ever intentionally force yourself to think about Christmas on the Fourth of July --- when the holiday season (calendar-wise) is farthest away? You get older, and the months between the red, white, and blue and the red, white and greed...er...GREEN, go by much more quickly. It was that way, again, for me this year. Does it seem that way for you too?

· · · · ·

Funny, but especially THIS year, everywhere I turn, I just want to cry --- yep, big ol', ugly dude like me. I've never seen so many people, for more reasons than ever, and for more reasons than I can count, hurting so badly, and it is truly worrisome that so many appear to be, at best, indifferent, or at worst, indignant. Have I for so long simply been "looking" and not really "seeing," or have we arrived at another honest to goodness "turning point" in history? If you have little ones these days, you already realize just how tough a task you face, as if it were not tough enough all along. My optimism, though, lies, as it must, in those same little ones, and the dedication/fortitude of those who guide them, to help save us from ourselves, for we have gotten woefully, woefully off-track.

· · · · ·

Most people don't like to discuss the topic, but I'm not most people. This reality never leaves my mind and helps me to better focus on all that truly matters in life. Every day, without fail, I contemplate my own MORTALITY --- the fact that I will not be here forever. One day, don't know when, you and the rest of the world will just have to get along without me. It is important that I create as many great memories as I can WHILE I can. And for as selfish as it must sound, I do this for ME. I realized long ago that great memories require great relationships. If I am to be happy --- relevant --- in this world, I need YOU. It's difficult to convince young people, but the time to create great memories is always right now. The opportunities, however, come and go in a flash. For all the evil that occurs all around us, there are always subtle "reminders" --- beautiful sunsets, brilliantly colored flowers, a diaper-clad toddler --- a dear friend's smile. These make the best vitamins. I continually remind myself that my blood type must be my attitude (B-positive). There will always be plenty to complain about, but none of that helps me find peace or fulfillment. It only reverses my Rh factor, and ushers in clouds and rain that drown my best fires. So, yes, I regularly think about not being here anymore. If I have been good at something, I am only reminding myself that my time is limited; my abilities are waning. My failures and shortcomings help me recognize my weaknesses --- my humanity. I try to make LESSONS of them. That way, no matter my age, I continue to grow. This message may worry some of you, but let me assure you, I am fine. My mother used to say I think too much. She was right about a lot of things.

· · · · ·

Knowing our time on earth is limited, we must get things done quickly while being careful to obey the speed limit signs posted along the way.

． ． ． ． ．

Do you shake your head when you hear young people repeat that oh-so-familiar line, "I can't wait 'til...?" Of course, they fill in the blank with all sorts of things. Older now, you realize just how fleeting this life is, don't you? Now it's you who repeat your own oh-so-familiar line --- "Oh my goodness, I've got to...!" Of course, you fill in the blank with all sorts of things. But now, wisdom rears ITS beautiful head, helping you to realize something truly profound. LIFE IS A RACE, BUT YOU SHOULDN'T RUSH IT. Most of the time, older people don't move slowly because they can't move faster. They move slowly --- walking, shopping, DRIVING --- because they know they'll get it done --- they know they'll get there...eventually.

． ． ． ． ．

Another growing old(er) realization: Learn to laugh at yourself. Some of the stuff you do will be absolutely hilarious! Made you think of an incident --- or two --- didn't I?

． ． ． ． ．

Ocean waves, fall leaves, wind, a field of flowers, snow --- have you ever witnessed a young animal --- colt, puppy, virtually any animal --- encounter these things (so taken for granted) for the very first time? Words like exuberant, inquisitive, joy, --- LIFE --- come to mind. They are blissfully unaware that they will not feel this way --- BE this way --- forever.

· · · · ·

Usually about the time we become "veteran" teenagers --- between 16 and 18 years --- something fascinating happens. That senior year of high school is gone in a BLUR! Almost as soon as you get used to the idea of being at the top of the food chain in high school, the usual senior activities --- prom and other final year stuff --- you find yourself in some auditorium, properly robed, and waiting to be called to the stage to receive your diploma --- cap & gown, class ring, graduation announcements, college acceptance (where applicable, and all so important just a short time earlier) now memories.

· · · · ·

That senior year SHOULD have taught you --- convinced you --- but it rarely does. TIME seems to take on a life of its own. It puts its foot down hard on your accelerator, and in a flash, careers are over; you've reached, say, your sixties, and, if possible, you retire. You realize those years of playing in the leaves, waves, wind, and flowers have gone by the wayside. Hard life or easy life --- however you view it --- that old adage is true, "TIME WAITS FOR NO MAN." You find yourself in front of a mirror and asking, "What have I done with my life? What REALLY matters? What difference have I made in things?"

· · · · ·

Those who grow old and grumpy often realize, too late, they WASTED their one opportunity to truly live --- failed to realize earlier that the secret to living is LOVING. THAT is the "secret path" back to the leaves, the wind, the waves, the flowers, the snow, and so much more. The pure joy of a new puppy in the snow is MULTIPLIED if it has its LITTER MATES with it! It makes sense to take care to eat well, exercise regularly --- take care of yourself --- so you can "love" better. TIME is the "ultimate treasure." We are each obliged to play by ITS rules --- within ITS parameters. From seconds to decades, you only get one lifeTIME. "Graduate" from "success" to SIGNIFICANCE by choosing to love (I know it can be tough sometimes). It's best to remain a puppy. In the long run, you might find it's more than worth it.

· · · · ·

It is interesting how, as we age, the REASONS why we look into mirrors (and the EMOTIONS that result) change so drastically.

· · · · ·

DECADES ago (in the 50s), I never thought this modifier could possibly last this long and still mean the exact same thing --- COOL. That's right, kiddies, your GRANDPARENTS used that one too, possibly INVENTED it!

· · · · ·

In your journey through life, it's good to be observant, watching closely all that goes on around you. It is equally important to keep one eye on yourself, not in self-admiration, but in a sincere, constant desire to set a proper example of how that journey should be traveled. That one goal is its own reward, and the best way to diminish (eliminate?) the fear of it all coming to an end, as it surely will. When it does come to an end, you should be smiling, and exhausted.

· · · · ·

When I was younger, I wondered how old people could speak so casually about death --- especially their own. Now, I understand completely.

· · · · ·

All of life is a huge test. When it's over --- once people announce that you've passed --- hopefully, they mean it BOTH ways.

· · · · ·

Enjoyed lunch with a bunch of guys recently --- former high school classmates. Funny how the main topic of discussion, when we were young dudes, was girls. Now, we sit around and compare surgical scars --- sad.

· · · · ·

Everyone wants to live a long life, but no one wants to grow old --- nothing new. When the years begin to add up, memory fades and joints creak, but perhaps worst of all, you begin to lose lots more friends and loved ones. Long life can be a mixed blessing.

· · · · ·

If you really want to know how fleeting this life is, ask a SENIOR --- makes sense.

· · · · ·

Going to one's "eternal rest", in a very real sense, is an appropriate term. Lived well, life is, and SHOULD be, exhausting. It's impossible to do the right thing all the time, and because there are always more than enough wrongs to right, that task is endless. Nevertheless, a life lived properly not only diminishes the fear of its end but also makes the inevitability of it almost welcome.

· · · · ·

At death, everyone knows the body literally turns to dust. How sad that so many of the LIVING are being treated as if they already are.

· · · · ·

How many times in your life has someone told you, "Hey, don't throw those away?" We have become such a "throwaway" society; everything is disposable, it seems. Among all the items we discard, it is unwise to include the elderly --- those who, in many ways, contribute so much to who we are today. Unlike plastics and aluminum, they are NOT recyclable.

· · · · ·

I forget names and can't remember where I leave things, but I think my BODY, despite my finest efforts, is aging faster than my MIND. I'm at that age where they, regularly, argue with each other. Thankfully, my mind usually wins.

· · · · ·

Most distance runners are familiar with the term, "splits." They divide a race distance into (not necessarily equal) parts and run a preset pace through those parts as if they were actually different races. Setting goals (and strategies to achieve them) is wise when it comes to improving performance. For example, a 1600-meter race might be divided into 4 parts of 400 meters, or perhaps 8 parts of 200 meters. As with anything else, experience pays huge dividends. Those who train hard and consistently can run "negative splits." They can run the earlier parts at a fast pace, and the latter parts even faster. They are almost always the best. They learn to deal with pain --- to "hurt better" --- than their competition. They know a fast early pace will likely elevate fear and doubt in those competitors who would prefer to start "slow and easy" in the useless hope of looking "good" as they sprint across the line only to finish next to last. LIFE and distance running have much in common.

· · · · ·

There's an old saying: "Your arms are too short to box with God." But there's another (undefeated) opponent in that ring --- TIME!

· · · · ·

I never could dunk a basketball, but back in the day, I could jump up and grab the rim. Now I trip over the free throw line.

· · · · ·

It doesn't matter whether they played professionally, or barely made the junior varsity team, long after the cheering stops and the fans have all gone home, athletes reach a point in life where they remember how they could (once upon a time) make their bodies do things they now find amazing --- great memories.

· · · · ·

My brain must be growing. My forehead is getting bigger!

· · · · ·

Old folks, for a variety of reasons, don't tell you (or never get the chance to), what a marvelous, wonder-filled blessing it is to grow old. Everyone notices the PHYSICAL changes, there are many, but few recognize a crucial irony. As their eyesight fades, their INSIGHT explodes in ways they cannot adequately explain. It is a terrible mistake to "box" those priceless volumes and store them away in attics to collect dust. To do so is to burn entire libraries.

· · · · ·

When life is lived selflessly --- with a focus on the welfare and betterment of family and friends (even strangers) --- time accelerates in amazing ways. Next thing you know, kids have grown up, you and your best friends have become grandparents, and those dreams of retirement become a reality. But gray hair should never mean just sitting on a porch, playing checkers, and watching the neighborhood kids play.

$$\cdot \ \cdot \ \cdot \ \cdot \ \cdot$$

Many have a "treasure room" --- a little shrine somewhere in the house to display tokens of former prowess: trophies, medals, plaques, certificates, documents --- souvenirs that declare (often loudly), that at some point in life, we mattered. The next time you pass a mirror, take a good, honest look. Of all things relevant in this life, what, in fact, have you done? In your own sphere of influence, what sacrifices have you made to better the lives of others? Therein lies the real treasure --- the source that reveals the difference between success and significance. It's really that simple. That is loving; that is LIFE.

$$\cdot \ \cdot \ \cdot \ \cdot \ \cdot$$

A message to my peers: Your coordination isn't what it once was. You stumble sometimes --- verbally, physically, and mentally --- and you drop things --- pills (that always roll under the couch or the fridge), cell phones (oh no!), and you are extra careful holding babies (usually while you're sitting). It could all be so depressing but know this. At your age, you've likely witnessed more change in this world than any prior generation --- countless events (great and small, wonderful and tragic), and mind-boggling technological advances. That makes YOU a priceless commodity --- the best library ever! (Your grandchildren already know this.) I hope you are surrounded by others who are smart enough to listen to what you have to say.

· · · · ·

Another "aging" revelation: It's fascinating how, when you are a seasoned adult, you just "know" stuff. You've been to lots of places, seen and done lots of things. Then, just when you think you've graduated from mere intelligence to genuine wisdom, nobody cares what you think, or wants to hear what you have to say.

· · · · ·

Just had a routine scan done at the hospital (when you get a certain age...). So, you lie back; they attach all that apparatus to you (hither and yon); and you watch and listen to those monster machines slowly hum, click, buzz, and whirr as they go about "checking you out." Quietly, you pray no alarms go off, but they seldom do, and in no time at all, you're up and out the door, hoping your insurance company picks up the tab. Your dentist, your veterinarian, and even the gym you (seldom) frequent all have these crazy, new machines (and they are constantly morphing)! You can't help feeling like a guinea pig. I miss my little wheel.

· · · · ·

So, at long last, you finally get your eyes done. You can SEE for the first time in decades, and then almost ruin it all poking yourself in the eye with your READING glasses! Are we having fun yet?

· · · · ·

The most dangerous truth --- too often forgotten --- is that being human also means being MORTAL.

· · · · ·

My Texas cousin, Donnie, and I are about the same age. We sometimes discuss the symptoms and challenges of aging. One of our favorites is starting a sentence, and then forgetting the rest of it --- often asking ourselves, "Was I finished?" We say it's like throwing a boomerang into the Grand Canyon. "That one ain't comin' back!"

· · · · ·

As we age, there is a term that once meant "boring." Now, it means "essential" --- ROUTINE.

. . . . .

Live long enough --- well enough --- and you will one day reach a point where you'll say to yourself, "I don't want to do this anymore. God, You take over" (as if He hadn't already).

. . . . .

Another handy "getting dressed" tip: After the shower, when you're putting on your underwear and your toes get caught in the leg opening, LET GO OF THE UNDERWEAR! If you hang on (after a few hopscotch moves), you might be near a bed or a soft chair. It is important to fall (if you must) in the RIGHT DIRECTION. (Yes, these instructions are the result of --- rather extensive --- experience.)

. . . . .

Once upon a time, it was driving too fast and partying too late --- dangerous. Now it's trying to put your pants on without holding onto something --- even MORE dangerous!

. . . . .

Live long enough, and you'll begin to understand truths so powerful that you will be humbled --- deeply moved. They manifest themselves in gray hair and wrinkles, but almost magically, you just "know" and begin to cherish what matters most in life. The world calls them "little things." Strangely, others may realize them, but they are meant to be shared with only a chosen few. Your failing vision is sharpened beyond 20-20; their ears learn to disregard the world's noise.

· · · · ·

Some of the most valuable gifts of aging involve "transitions." Looking morphs into seeing; speculation, into fact (reality) --- intelligence, into wisdom. However, before wisdom can be realized, attention must be paid to the lessons of history. After so much experience, how can we remain so oblivious to the fact that love ALWAYS works better than hate? Some will remember how record players (explain to the "younger set") used to "skip" and replay the same section of those old, worn tunes. Lesson: the "genre" of the music never really matters at all.

· · · · ·

Youth is something. Remember when you could leave the house at 10 p.m., party all night, get back home, shower, get dressed, go to work the next day, and not miss a beat? Old athletes think like that too. Remember when you could...? Old age is something!

· · · · ·

When life is lived selflessly --- with a focus on the welfare and betterment of family and friends (even strangers) --- time accelerates in amazing ways. Next thing you know, kids have grown up, you and your best friends have become grandparents, and those dreams of retirement become a reality. But gray hair should never mean sitting on a porch, playing checkers, and watching the neighborhood kids play.

· · · · ·

As a bona-fide senior citizen, I look back and realize the incredible period in history I have been blessed to witness. For, as amazing as it has all been, it has not been easy. I grew up in the greatest of countries, but as a Black man, it has not been without its "extra" challenges. The trials have been many, and I often find myself getting so caught up in my own struggles that I forget those of the many who came before me. Then, I realize I have no right to complain. By comparison, what is my mere fatigue - disappointment – frustration compared to the unimaginable suffering endured by my ancestors? I am fine, thank you, and despite my years, I have a little grit left and I fully intend to fight to the end.

Author Biography

Dr. Jerry Gaines, a life-long educator, began his career in 1972 at Western Branch High School in Chesapeake, Virginia where he taught and coached for twenty-one years. He spent the next fifteen years as a high school assistant principal (three at the Chesapeake Center for Science and Technology, and twelve at Great Bridge High). He completed the last three years of his career as a Central Office Supervisor.

Notable achievements include his selection as Teacher of the Year for the Chesapeake School System, Coach of the Year by the Portsmouth Sports Club, being inducted into the Hampton Roads African American Sports Hall of Fame and inducted into the Hall of Legends by the Chesapeake Sports Club. Dr. Gaines was the first Black Athlete to earn a full athletic scholarship to Virginia Tech where he still holds two records in track & field. He is also the first Black Athlete to be inducted into the school's Sports Hall of Fame. After college, toward the end of the Vietnam war, he served his country honorably as an officer in the U.S. Army. In 2023, VA Tech honored him by dedicating the VT Director of Track and Field Office to Dr. Gaines.

While working as an educator, Dr. Gaines used his love of fishing to reach out and mentor young people he came to know and love. Many of the relationships that developed have lasted more than 50 years. To this day he takes great joy in meeting with former students, catching up on what is happening in their lives, and developing new relationships with their families!

After retiring as an educator, Dr. Gaines traveled the country sharing a very profound message that he claims, "a million kids taught HIM." As a tribute to those many lives that he has touched, he has written a book entitled "40 Stories High" – a selection of short stories recounting some of his most moving experiences teaching, coaching, and mentoring.

More recently, Dr. Gaines tries to keep his speaking engagements within a short drive from his home. He still gets out his fishing rods as much as possible, often accompanied by former students who just need a bit of "Gaines Time"! His greatest joy is his granddaughters, and he delights in being a part of their lives.

www.ingramcontent.com/pod-product-compliance
Lightning Source LLC
Chambersburg PA
CBHW051134120626
46547CB00012B/802